# MAURITIUS TRAVEL GUIDE

## 2024 Edition

Exploring Paradise: Your Ultimate Mauritius Travel Companion

**Jim Baxter**

All rights reserved. No part of this book may be reproduced, stored in a retrieval system, or transmitted in any form or by any means, electronic, mechanical, photocopying, recording, or otherwise, without the prior written permission of the copyright owner. The information contained in this book is for general information purposes only. The author and publisher make no representations or warranties of any kind, express or implied, about the completeness, accuracy, reliability, suitability or availability with respect to the book or the information, products, services, or related graphics contained in the book for any purpose. Any reliance you place on such information is therefore strictly at your own risk.

Copyright © 2023 by Jim Baxter.

# TABLE OF CONTENT

*Introduction* _____ 7
   **Welcome to Mauritius** _____ 9
   **Why Visit Mauritius?** _____ 11
   **Getting to Know the Island** _____ 14

*Chapter 1: Essential Travel Planning* _____ 19
   **When to Go: Best Time to Visit** _____ 19
   **Entry Requirements and Visa Information** ____ 23
   **Health and Safety Precautions** _____ 27
   **Currency and Financial Tips** _____ 31

*Chapter 2: Navigating Mauritius* _____ 37
   **Getting Around the Island** _____ 37
      Renting a Car: Exploring Mauritius at Your Own Pace 37
      Public Buses in Mauritius: Affordable and Comprehensive Transportation _____ 41
      Taxis: Your Convenient Mode of Transport _____ 43
      Cycling in Mauritius: Embracing Eco-Friendly Exploration _____ 46
      Walking Tours: Exploring Port Louis and Grand Baie on Foot _____ 49

   **Language and Communication** _____ 52

*Chapter 3: Island Regions and Their Charms* ____ 59
   **Exploring Port Louis: The Capital City** _____ 59
   **Grand Baie: A Hub of Entertainment and Shopping** _____ 63
   **Cultural Treasures of Mahebourg** _____ 66
   **Tranquility of Rodrigues Island** _____ 71
   **Chamarel and the Southwest Coast** _____ 75

Flic-en-Flac and the West Coast _____79

*Chapter 4: Where to Stay* _____85

Luxury Resorts and Boutique Hotels _____85

Budget-Friendly Accommodations _____89

Unique Stays: Villas and Guesthouses _____93

*Chapter 5: Savoring Mauritian Cuisine* _____97

A Culinary Fusion: Influences and Flavors _____97

Must-Try Dishes and Street Food _____100

Dining Etiquette and Tips _____106

*Chapter 6: Immerse in Culture and History* _____111

Heritage Sites and Museums _____111

Aapravasi Ghat: A Testament to Resilience and History _____111

Eureka House: A Glimpse into Colonial Opulence _____113

Château de Labourdonnais: Unraveling the Sugar Plantation Era _____114

Blue Penny Museum: A Philatelic and Cultural Treasure _____116

Traditional Music, Dance, and Festivals _____117

Learning About the Island's History _____124

*Chapter 7: Breathtaking Natural Wonders* _____131

Beaches of Paradise: White Sands and Azure Waters _____131

Exploring Coral Reefs and Marine Life _____137

Discovering the Inner Beauty: Waterfalls and Hiking Trails _____139

The Mystical Chamarel Colored Earths _____142

Underwater Waterfall Illusion at Le Morne _____144

Ile aux Aigrettes: A Conservation Success Story....146

*Chapter 8: Adventure Awaits* _____149

   Water Sports and Activities: Snorkeling, Diving, and Surfing _____149

   Exploring National Parks and Wildlife Reserves _____154

   Adrenaline-Pumping Adventures: Zip-lining, Quad Biking, and More _____157

*Chapter 9: Shopping and Souvenirs* _____161

   Local Markets and Handicrafts _____161

   Where to Find Authentic Souvenirs _____165

   Sustainable Shopping: Supporting Local Artisans _____169

*Chapter 10: Travel Itineraries* _____173

   Family friendly itinerary _____173

   5-day travel Itinerary _____184

   7-day Travel itinerary _____193

*Conclusion* _____201

   Appendix A: Useful Phrases in Mauritian Creole _____203

   Appendix B: Traveler's Checklist _____207

   Appendix C: Recommended Reading and Resources _____209

# Important Note Before You Continue Reading

Unlock a World of Wonder: Embrace the Uncharted Beauty of Mauritius

Step into a realm where extraordinary experiences lie within the pages of this exceptional travel guide. Our mission is simple: to ignite your imagination, fuel your creativity, and awaken the daring adventurer within you. Unlike conventional guides, we choose to forgo images, as we firmly believe in the power of firsthand discovery—unfiltered and uninfluenced by preconceptions. Prepare yourself for an enchanting voyage, where each monument, every corner, and every hidden gem eagerly await your personal encounter. Why spoil the exhilaration of that first glimpse, that overwhelming sense of awe? Get ready to embark on an unparalleled journey, where the vessel propelling you forward is none other than your boundless imagination, and you will be the architect of your own destiny. Abandon any preconceived notions and find yourself transported to an authentic Mauritian experience, a realm teeming with extraordinary revelations. Brace yourself, for the magic of this expedition begins now, and remember, the most breathtaking images will be the ones painted by your own eyes.

In stark contrast to traditional guides, this book rejects the need for detailed maps. Why, you ask? Because we fervently believe that the greatest discoveries occur when you lose yourself, when you surrender to the ebb and flow of your surroundings, and embrace the thrill of the unknown path. No predetermined itineraries, no precise directions—our intention is to liberate you, allowing you to explore Mauritius on your terms, without boundaries or limitations. Surrender to the currents and unveil hidden treasures that no map could ever reveal. Embrace audacity, follow your instincts, and prepare to be astounded. The magic of this expedition commences in your world without maps, where roads materialize with each step, and the most extraordinary adventures await within the unexplored folds of the unknown.

# Introduction

Mauritius, an enchanting gem nestled in the vast expanse of the Indian Ocean, beckons travelers with its irresistible blend of natural beauty, cultural richness, and a warm, welcoming atmosphere. Its allure lies not only in its pristine beaches and crystal-clear waters but also in the vibrant tapestry of traditions, flavors, and experiences that define this paradise. This introduction sets the stage for your journey through this captivating destination, offering profound insight into why Mauritius is a must-visit and providing an alluring glimpse into the island's unique character.

**A Jewel in the Indian Ocean**

Picture yourself standing on the shore, feeling the fine grains of sand underfoot, and gazing out at the endless expanse of the Indian Ocean. Mauritius, often referred to as the "Jewel of the Indian Ocean," is a treasure trove of natural wonders that seem almost too perfect to be real. Turquoise lagoons, fringed by lush palm trees, paint a vivid contrast against the sapphire hues of the sea. It's a place where the sunsets are a daily masterpiece, and the gentle trade winds carry the tantalizing scent of tropical blooms.

But Mauritius is more than just an idyllic postcard destination. It's a living testament to the harmony that can exist between nature and humanity. Here, the land has been sculpted into vibrant gardens, pristine parks, and verdant forests, all coexisting in perfect equilibrium. Coral reefs, teeming with life, serve as a reminder of the delicate ecosystems that thrive beneath the ocean's surface. It's a place where nature's beauty is not just admired but revered and protected.

## A Tapestry of Cultures

Beyond its natural splendors, Mauritius boasts a rich tapestry of cultures and traditions that weave together to create a vibrant and harmonious society. The island's history is a tale of exploration, colonization, and migration, resulting in a unique blend of influences that is unlike anywhere else on Earth.

You'll discover the flavors of India, France, China, and Africa mingling in the aromas of Mauritian cuisine. You'll witness the joyful celebrations of Diwali, Eid, Christmas, and Chinese New Year, each adding its own color to the cultural mosaic. And as you traverse the island, you'll be welcomed by the warm smiles and open hearts of the Mauritian people, whose friendliness and hospitality are legendary.

## A Must-Visit Destination

Mauritius isn't just a destination; it's an experience waiting to be embraced. Whether you seek adventure on the hiking trails that crisscross the island's interior, relaxation on a pristine beach, or a deep dive into the island's history and culture, Mauritius has something to offer every traveler.

In the chapters that follow, we will be your guide through this extraordinary island, helping you uncover its hidden gems, navigate its diverse regions, and immerse yourself in its culture and natural wonders. From the bustling streets of Port Louis, the capital city, to the tranquil shores of Rodrigues Island, we will unravel the secrets of Mauritius so you can make the most of your journey.

So, fasten your seatbelts and prepare for an unforgettable expedition through Mauritius, where paradise meets reality and every moment is a cherished memory in the making.

# Welcome to Mauritius

As you step off the plane and onto the tarmac of Sir Seewoosagur Ramgoolam International Airport, you are immediately enveloped in an atmosphere of tranquility and beauty. A gentle, balmy breeze carries with it the intoxicating fragrance of frangipani blossoms, a scent that instantly awakens your senses to the fact that you have arrived in a place like no other. Welcome to Mauritius, a destination that effortlessly casts a spell on visitors with its paradisiacal landscapes and the genuine warmth of its people.

Mauritius, often referred to as the "Star and Key of the Indian Ocean," is a small island nation that boasts an extraordinary blend of natural wonders and cultural richness. Despite its relatively diminutive size on the world map, this island packs an impressive punch when it comes to offering a diverse range of experiences.

One of the island's most celebrated features is its pristine beaches. These idyllic shores, adorned with powdery white sands that stretch as far as the eye can see, are gently caressed by the turquoise waters of the Indian Ocean. It's here that you can recline beneath the shade of swaying palm trees, your toes sinking into the soft sand, as you soak up the sun's warm embrace. Whether you seek solitude or the vibrant buzz of beachside activities, Mauritius has a coastline to suit your desires.

Beyond the beaches, Mauritius hides lush forests and verdant landscapes, home to a rich tapestry of flora and fauna. Tropical rainforests teem with life, and you might spot rare bird species, vibrant butterflies, or even curious monkeys as you venture into these pristine natural habitats. The island's interior is a playground for hikers and nature enthusiasts, with hiking trails that lead to cascading waterfalls, panoramic viewpoints, and hidden gems waiting to be discovered.

Yet, what truly sets Mauritius apart is its vibrant cultural tapestry. Influenced by centuries of history and the convergence of diverse ethnicities, the island's culture is a captivating blend of Indian, African, French, and British heritage. This amalgamation has given rise to a unique way of life, a harmonious coexistence of traditions, and a culinary scene that's a delightful fusion of flavors and techniques. From savoring mouthwatering Creole dishes in local eateries to participating in lively Sega dance performances during festivals, your journey through Mauritius will be a cultural immersion like no other.

In this travel guide, we're thrilled to accompany you on an exploration of this exquisite island. Our aim is to unveil the hidden treasures of Mauritius while providing you with practical insights that will make your trip truly unforgettable. From the vibrant streets of Port Louis, where the past and present merge seamlessly, to the tranquil and secluded shores of Rodrigues, each chapter will reveal the diversity and beauty that make Mauritius a genuine tropical paradise. Whether you're an adventure seeker, a nature lover, a culture enthusiast, or simply in search of a tranquil escape, Mauritius has something magical in store for you. So, let's embark on this journey together, and let the allure of Mauritius capture your heart and soul.

## Why Visit Mauritius?

"Why Mauritius?" you might ask. The reasons are as numerous as the grains of sand on its beaches, and each one is a compelling invitation to explore this remarkable island. Let's dive deeper into these reasons:

**Natural Beauty:**

Mauritius is a canvas painted with nature's finest hues. Its beaches are postcard-perfect, with powdery white sands caressed by the gentle waves of the Indian Ocean. Turquoise waters stretch as far as the eye can see, inviting you to swim, snorkel, or simply bask in the sun's warm embrace.

But it's not just the beaches that make Mauritius a natural wonder. Beneath the surface, coral reefs teem with vibrant marine life. Grab a snorkel and mask, and you'll enter a world of kaleidoscopic fish, graceful sea turtles, and intricate coral formations. For the more adventurous, scuba diving unveils even more secrets of the ocean's depths.

Venture inland, and you'll discover a lush interior adorned with cascading waterfalls and emerald-hued national parks. Hike through the Black River Gorges National Park, where lush rainforests give way to sweeping viewpoints, or chase waterfalls like Chamarel and Alexandra Falls, which tumble dramatically through the verdant terrain. Nature enthusiasts, photographers, and eco-lovers will find paradise within these landscapes.

**Cultural Melting Pot:**

Mauritius isn't just a feast for the eyes; it's a cultural smorgasbord for the soul. The island's multicultural heritage is a testament to its history, where African, Indian, French, and British influences have converged into a harmonious fusion.

Cultural enthusiasts can savor the diverse cuisine, a tantalizing blend of flavors from around the world, with Creole dishes taking center stage. Tantalize your taste buds with fragrant curries, spicy rougailles, and delectable seafood dishes prepared with a hint of French finesse.

Throughout the year, Mauritius comes alive with vibrant festivals that celebrate its rich heritage. From Diwali, the Festival of Lights, to Chinese New Year and the lively Sega dance performances, you'll have the opportunity to immerse yourself in the island's traditions.

Historic sites and museums beckon those eager to uncover the island's past. Visit places like Aapravasi Ghat, a UNESCO World Heritage Site, which tells the story of indentured laborers who arrived on the island, or explore the colonial architecture of Port Louis, offering glimpses into its colonial history.

**Water Sports Galore:**

For water lovers, Mauritius is a playground that doesn't disappoint. The warm, crystal-clear waters invite you to explore their depths. Snorkeling is a must, and even novice snorkelers can marvel at the vibrant coral gardens and aquatic life just beneath the surface.

For the adventurous, there's kite surfing, windsurfing, and paddleboarding. The consistent trade winds create ideal conditions for these exhilarating sports. Whether you're a seasoned pro or a beginner looking to try something new, Mauritius offers the perfect environment for aquatic adventures.

**Luxurious Retreats:**

Mauritius understands the art of pampering like few other places. The island is dotted with world-class resorts and accommodations that redefine luxury. Imagine waking up to the soothing sounds of the ocean, with a private beach just steps from your doorstep. Many resorts offer overwater bungalows where you can dive into the sea from your deck or unwind in a private infinity pool while gazing at the Indian Ocean.

Spa enthusiasts can indulge in a range of treatments, often inspired by local ingredients and traditions. Relax with a massage under swaying palm trees or in a serene spa overlooking the pristine beaches.

**Adventure and Exploration:**

For those seeking an adrenaline rush, Mauritius is an adventure playground. The rugged interior of the island begs to be explored, and there are numerous ways to do it. Strap on your hiking boots and trek through lush forests, scaling peaks for breathtaking panoramic views. Quad biking adventures take you off-road, winding through sugar cane fields and to hidden waterfalls.

If you're a thrill-seeker, try zip-lining through the treetops or canyoning down waterfalls. The possibilities for adventure are as diverse as the island itself.

In Mauritius, every day is an opportunity for a new adventure, a cultural discovery, or a moment of pure relaxation. This island, with its natural beauty, rich culture, and endless activities, invites you to embrace its charms and create memories that will last a lifetime.

# Getting to Know the Island

Before embarking on your adventure, it's essential to understand the geography, climate, and culture of Mauritius.

This knowledge will not only enhance your travel experience but also help you make informed choices during your stay.

## Geography of Mauritius

Mauritius is a volcanic island located approximately 2,000 kilometers off the southeast coast of Africa. It forms part of the Mascarene Islands, which include nearby Réunion and Rodrigues. Despite its relatively small size, covering an area of about 2,040 square kilometers, Mauritius boasts a diverse landscape that will leave you awestruck.

The island is renowned for its stunning beaches, fringed with palm trees and lapped by crystal-clear waters. However, venture inland, and you'll discover a world of contrasts. Towering peaks, such as the iconic Le Morne Brabant and the lush Black River Gorges, dominate the interior. These volcanic remnants offer excellent hiking opportunities and panoramic vistas of the island's lush greenery.

Mauritius is surrounded by coral reefs, creating serene lagoons that are perfect for swimming, snorkeling, and diving. The island's geography is also responsible for its favorable climate, with warm temperatures year-round. However, it's crucial to be aware of the island's seasons to plan your visit effectively.

## Climate in Mauritius

Mauritius enjoys a tropical climate characterized by two main seasons: a wet season and a dry season. The wet season typically runs from November to April, marked by occasional heavy rainfall, high humidity, and the risk of cyclones. This period is ideal for those interested in lush green landscapes and waterfalls at their fullest. The wet season is also when the island's flora is in full bloom, adding to the scenic beauty.

Conversely, the dry season, which occurs from May to October, offers cooler, drier weather. This is the peak tourist season when the island experiences less rainfall, lower humidity, and milder temperatures. These conditions make it ideal for outdoor activities like hiking, snorkeling, and beach relaxation.

**Culture and People of Mauritius**

Mauritius is often celebrated as a harmonious tapestry of cultures. The island's history is shaped by a rich blend of Indian, African, French, and British influences, which are reflected in its customs, traditions, and cuisine.

The population of Mauritius is remarkably diverse, with various ethnic groups coexisting peacefully. Indo-Mauritians, Creole-Mauritians, Sino-Mauritians, and Franco-Mauritians are among the prominent communities, each contributing to the island's cultural mosaic. This diversity is celebrated through festivals, music, dance, and a wide range of culinary delights, ensuring that every corner of Mauritius is a cultural experience waiting to be explored.

While English and French are the official languages, you'll find that Mauritian Creole is the language of everyday communication among the locals. Learning a few basic Creole phrases can go a long way in enhancing your interactions and immersing yourself in the local culture.

Understanding these aspects of Mauritius—its geography, climate, and culture—will serve as a solid foundation for your exploration of this tropical paradise. It will not only enrich your travel experience but also enable you to make informed decisions throughout your stay, ensuring that your journey through Mauritius is as enjoyable as it is enlightening.

As you read on, you'll delve deeper into these aspects and gain a comprehensive understanding of Mauritius, ensuring that your journey through this island paradise is both enjoyable and enriching.

# Chapter 1: Essential Travel Planning

Welcome to the first chapter of your Mauritius adventure! Before you embark on your journey to this tropical paradise, it's crucial to have a solid plan in place. This chapter will guide you through the essential aspects of travel planning for Mauritius, ensuring a smooth and enjoyable trip.

## When to Go: Best Time to Visit

Mauritius boasts a delightful tropical climate that attracts travelers from all corners of the globe. Whether you seek sun-soaked beaches, water adventures, or cultural exploration, understanding the island's climate and its seasonal nuances is pivotal in planning an unforgettable trip. In this section, we'll delve deeper into Mauritius' climate, exploring the different seasons and their unique characteristics to help you choose the best time to visit based on your preferences and interests.

**Dry Season (May to December): Ideal for Outdoor Enthusiasts**

The dry season in Mauritius, spanning from May to December, is a dream come true for outdoor enthusiasts. This period is characterized by lower humidity, abundant sunshine, and minimal rainfall, making it the go-to time for a wide array of activities.

Weather Conditions:

- Temperature: During the dry season, the temperature in Mauritius hovers around a comfortable 24°C to 30°C (75°F to 86°F). This mild climate creates the perfect backdrop for your adventures.

- Sunshine: Expect plenty of sunshine with blue skies. The consistent sunny weather is perfect for beach lovers, water sports, and exploring the island's natural wonders.

**Why Visit During the Dry Season:**

- Outdoor Activities: With the pleasant weather, this season is tailor-made for outdoor activities. You can indulge in snorkeling, diving, hiking, and golfing with ease.

- Peak Tourist Season: The dry season marks the peak tourist season in Mauritius. While this means more crowds, it also signifies a vibrant atmosphere, bustling events, and a wide range of accommodations and dining options.

- Whale Watching: If you're interested in observing majestic humpback whales, plan your visit from June to October when they migrate to Mauritian waters.

## Wet Season (January to April): Embrace the Lush Greenery

Mauritius' wet season, from January to April, ushers in a different facet of the island's beauty. While this period experiences occasional heavy rainfall and higher humidity, it's a time when Mauritius turns into a lush, green paradise.

Weather Conditions:

- **Temperature:** Temperatures during the wet season range from 25°C to 33°C (77°F to 91°F), offering a warm tropical experience.

- **Rainfall:** Be prepared for intermittent heavy rainfall, particularly in January and February. These downpours replenish the island's reservoirs and maintain its natural beauty.

## Why Visit During the Wet Season:

- **Lower Prices:** If you're looking for budget-friendly options, the wet season typically offers lower prices for accommodations and activities. You can enjoy Mauritius without breaking the bank.

- **Refreshing Showers:** While rainfall is more frequent, it usually occurs in short, heavy showers. If you don't mind occasional rain, you'll appreciate the refreshing breaks and the vibrant, green landscapes.

- Fewer Crowds: The wet season sees fewer tourists, which means quieter beaches, shorter queues, and more intimate experiences at popular attractions.

## Shoulder Seasons (April-May and September-December): Best of Both Worlds

The shoulder seasons, bridging the gap between the dry and wet seasons, provide a balance between pleasant weather and fewer crowds. These periods, from April to May and September to December, offer a unique Mauritius experience.

Weather Conditions:

- Temperature: Expect temperatures ranging from 22°C to 28°C (72°F to 82°F), providing a comfortable climate for exploration.

- Weather Variation: During the shoulder seasons, you might encounter a mix of sunny days and occasional rainfall. It's a transitional period, so be prepared for some variability.

## Why Visit During the Shoulder Seasons:

- Balanced Weather: These seasons offer a pleasant climate, suitable for various activities. You can enjoy the beaches, go hiking, or explore cultural sites without extreme weather conditions.

- Quieter Atmosphere: While not as crowded as the dry season, the shoulder seasons provide a more tranquil experience. It's an excellent time for travelers who prefer a peaceful vacation.

- Favorable Rates: Accommodation and activity prices may be more reasonable than during the peak season, allowing you to enjoy a cost-effective vacation.

In conclusion, Mauritius welcomes travelers year-round, and the best time to visit depends on your preferences. Whether you seek outdoor adventures, vibrant crowds, lush greenery, or tranquility, understanding the island's seasons will help you plan a trip that aligns perfectly with your desires.

# Entry Requirements and Visa Information

**Passport Requirements:** Ensure your passport is valid for at least six months beyond your planned departure date.

Your passport is your gateway to Mauritius, and its validity is crucial. To ensure a hassle-free entry into the country, make sure your passport meets the following requirements:

- Validity Period: Your passport should be valid for at least six months beyond your planned departure date from Mauritius. This requirement is essential to account for any unexpected delays or extensions during your stay.

- Blank Pages: Check that your passport has a sufficient number of blank pages for entry and exit stamps. A minimum of two to four blank pages is generally recommended.

- Damaged Passports: Ensure your passport is in good condition, without significant damage. Damaged passports might not be accepted by immigration authorities.

- Visa Pages: If you have acquired visas for other countries within your current passport, verify that you have enough visa pages available for Mauritius. Some visas can take up a full page.

- Renewal: If your passport is close to its expiration date, consider renewing it before your trip to Mauritius. Passport renewal processing times vary by country, so plan accordingly.

- Passport Copies: Make photocopies of your passport's main page and any visas you may have. Keep these copies in a separate place from your actual passport. Having extra copies can be invaluable in case your passport is lost or stolen.

**Visa Information:** Mauritius offers visa-free entry to many countries for stays of up to 90 days. Check the specific requirements for your nationality and ensure you meet them.

Mauritius has a liberal visa policy, allowing travelers from numerous countries to enter without a visa for short stays. Here's what you need to know:

- Visa-Free Countries: Mauritius grants visa-free entry for varying durations (usually up to 90 days) to citizens of many countries. Commonly, tourists from North America, Europe, and neighboring African countries can enter Mauritius without a visa.

- Duration of Stay: The length of your permitted stay may vary based on your nationality, so check the specific regulations that apply to you. It's essential to respect the authorized duration of your stay, as overstaying can result in fines or deportation.

- Visa Extensions: If you plan to stay beyond the initial visa-free period, inquire about the possibility of extending your stay with the Passport and Immigration Office in Mauritius. Extensions are typically granted for valid reasons, such as family visits or business purposes.

- Transit Passengers: Even if you're transiting through Mauritius and not staying overnight, it's advisable to confirm whether you need a transit visa based on your nationality.

- Work or Study Visas: If your visit involves work, study, or other non-tourist activities, you will likely need a specific visa. It's crucial to apply for the correct visa type before your arrival.

- Application Process: For travelers who do require a visa, start the application process well in advance. Contact the nearest Mauritian embassy or consulate for guidance on visa requirements, processing times, and application forms.

**Customs and Immigration:** Familiarize yourself with the customs regulations and immigration procedures for a smooth entry into Mauritius.

Upon arriving in Mauritius, you will go through customs and immigration procedures. Familiarizing yourself with these processes will help ensure a seamless entry:

- Customs Declarations: Fill out the required customs declaration forms honestly and accurately. Declare any items or goods you're bringing into the country that exceed the duty-free allowances.

- Duty-Free Allowances: Mauritius has specific duty-free allowances for items such as alcohol, tobacco, and personal effects. Exceeding these limits may result in customs duties.

- Restricted and Prohibited Items: Be aware of items that are restricted or prohibited in Mauritius. This can include certain foods, plants, and drugs. Bringing such items without proper authorization can lead to fines or confiscation.

- Health Declarations: In light of health concerns such as the COVID-19 pandemic, be prepared to provide health-related information, including vaccination records or test results, if required.

- Immigration Procedures: Expect to undergo passport and visa checks by immigration officers. Have your travel documents, including your passport and any necessary visas, readily accessible.

- Customs Inspections: Random inspections of baggage may occur. Cooperation with customs and immigration authorities is essential for a smooth entry process.

- Departure Procedures: Familiarize yourself with the departure procedures for when you're leaving Mauritius. Ensure you have all necessary documents, including exit visas if applicable.

By ensuring that your passport is in order, understanding Mauritius' visa requirements for your nationality, and being knowledgeable about customs and immigration procedures, you'll set the foundation for a hassle-free and enjoyable visit to this stunning island nation. Remember to check for any updates or changes to these requirements before your departure to stay well-prepared.

## Health and Safety Precautions

Ensuring your well-being during your journey to Mauritius is paramount. This island paradise offers an incredible array of experiences, but understanding how to safeguard your health and safety is essential for a worry-free trip. This section provides valuable information on staying healthy and safe in Mauritius:

**Vaccinations: Learn about recommended and required vaccinations before traveling to Mauritius.**

Before setting foot on Mauritian soil, it's crucial to be aware of the vaccination requirements and recommendations for your trip. While Mauritius is relatively low-risk for many diseases, taking preventive measures can provide you with peace of mind during your stay.

- Routine Vaccinations: Ensure your routine vaccinations are up-to-date. This includes vaccines for diseases like measles, mumps, rubella, and diphtheria.

- Hepatitis A and Typhoid: These vaccines are usually recommended for travelers to Mauritius, as food and waterborne illnesses can occur.

- Yellow Fever: If you're arriving from a country with a risk of yellow fever transmission, you may need to provide proof of vaccination.

- Other Vaccinations: Depending on your travel plans and medical history, your healthcare provider may recommend additional vaccines, such as hepatitis B or rabies.

It's advisable to consult a healthcare professional or a travel clinic well in advance of your trip to determine the specific vaccinations you need. Make sure you receive vaccinations at least a few weeks before departure to allow your body to build immunity.

**Healthcare Facilities: Discover the quality of healthcare services on the island and how to access medical assistance if needed.**

- Mauritius boasts a relatively high standard of healthcare services. The country has both public and private healthcare facilities, with the latter often offering better amenities and shorter waiting times.

- Public Healthcare: Mauritius has a public healthcare system that provides basic medical services to residents and visitors. While these facilities are generally adequate for minor illnesses and injuries, they may lack some of the advanced equipment and services found in private hospitals.

- Private Healthcare: Private healthcare facilities in Mauritius are of a higher standard and are well-equipped to handle various medical situations. Hospitals such as the Apollo Bramwell Hospital and the Fortis Clinique Darné offer excellent medical care. It's advisable to have comprehensive travel insurance that covers medical expenses, as healthcare in private facilities can be costly.

- Pharmacies: Pharmacies are readily available in towns and tourist areas. They usually stock a wide range of medications, and the pharmacists are knowledgeable and helpful. For minor ailments, you can often obtain over-the-counter medications without a prescription.

- Emergency Services: In case of a medical emergency, dial 114 for an ambulance. Emergency services are generally responsive and efficient.

**Safety Tips: Get insights into safety precautions, such as avoiding petty theft and respecting local customs.**

While Mauritius is a relatively safe destination for travelers, it's essential to take precautions to ensure your safety and respect the local culture:

- Petty Theft: Like in many tourist destinations, petty theft can be a concern, especially in crowded areas and public transportation. To protect yourself, keep your valuables secure, avoid displaying expensive items, and be cautious when in busy tourist spots.

- Water Safety: Mauritius offers numerous opportunities for water-based activities. While enjoying the ocean, follow safety guidelines, and adhere to the instructions of lifeguards. Be cautious of strong currents and tides, especially in areas like Le Morne.

- Respect Local Customs: Mauritius is a diverse and culturally rich nation. Respect local customs, traditions, and dress codes, especially when visiting religious sites. Dress modestly when required, remove your shoes when entering temples, and ask for permission before taking photos of locals.

- Driving Safety: If you plan to rent a vehicle, be aware that Mauritius follows left-hand driving. Familiarize yourself with local traffic rules and drive cautiously, especially on winding coastal roads.

- Health Precautions: To stay healthy during your trip, drink bottled water, avoid consuming street food from unhygienic sources, and use sunscreen to protect yourself from the sun's strong rays.

By following these safety tips and staying informed about local customs and healthcare facilities, you can enhance your overall experience in Mauritius while prioritizing your well-being throughout your journey. Remember that responsible travel contributes to the preservation of this beautiful island and its unique culture.

# Currency and Financial Tips

Effective financial management is a cornerstone of any successful travel experience, and Mauritius is no exception.

This section provides you with crucial insights into understanding the local currency, managing your expenses, and ensuring a hassle-free financial journey during your visit to this tropical paradise.

**Mauritian Rupee (MUR): Learn about the currency, its denominations, and where to exchange money.**

The official currency of Mauritius is the Mauritian Rupee (MUR). Understanding the currency and its denominations is essential for a smooth financial transaction experience while you're in Mauritius.

- Denominations: The Mauritian Rupee is divided into smaller units, with coins in denominations of 5, 20, and 50 cents, and banknotes in denominations of 25, 50, 100, 200, 500, and 2,000 Rupees. Familiarize yourself with the various denominations to make handling money more convenient.

- Currency Exchange: Before you depart for Mauritius, it's advisable to exchange some currency in your home country. International airports and hotels in Mauritius also offer currency exchange services, but these may have less favorable exchange rates and higher fees. Banks and currency exchange offices in major cities like Port Louis typically provide better rates and lower fees.

- ATMs: ATMs are widely available in Mauritius, especially in urban areas and popular tourist destinations. They dispense Mauritian Rupees, and

many accept major international credit and debit cards. Keep in mind that while ATMs are generally convenient, they may charge withdrawal fees, so check with your home bank regarding any international transaction fees before using them.
- Currency Conversion Apps: Download a currency conversion app to your smartphone. This handy tool will help you quickly calculate the value of items in your home currency, making it easier to understand costs and expenses.

**Credit Cards and ATMs: Discover the availability of ATMs and the acceptance of credit cards across the island.**

Understanding the availability of ATMs and credit card acceptance in Mauritius is vital for managing your finances efficiently.

- Credit Cards: Credit cards, especially Visa and Mastercard, are widely accepted at hotels, upscale restaurants, and larger stores. However, it's wise to carry some cash for smaller establishments and in more remote areas where card acceptance might be limited.

- ATMs: As mentioned earlier, ATMs are readily available in Mauritius, making it easy to withdraw cash when needed. Most ATMs provide instructions in multiple languages, including English and French.

- Notify Your Bank: Before traveling, notify your bank of your travel plans to prevent your card from being flagged for suspicious activity. This will ensure uninterrupted access to your funds while abroad.

- Currency Conversion Fees: Be aware that some banks and credit card companies charge currency conversion fees for foreign transactions. Research and choose cards that offer favorable exchange rates and lower fees if you plan to use cards frequently.

**Budgeting: Get tips on managing your expenses and creating a travel budget tailored to your preferences.**

Budgeting is a fundamental aspect of a successful trip. Here are some tips for managing your expenses and creating a travel budget that aligns with your preferences:

- Set a Daily Allowance: Determine how much you're comfortable spending per day, factoring in accommodations, meals, activities, and souvenirs. Having a daily allowance in mind helps you stay on track.

- Prioritize Spending: Identify the experiences and activities that are most important to you. Allocate a larger portion of your budget to these priorities and be more conservative with less essential expenses.

- Keep Records: Maintain a record of your expenditures. This can be as simple as jotting down what you spend in a notebook or using a budgeting app. Tracking your expenses helps you stay within your budget and identify areas where you can save.

- Emergency Fund: Include a portion of your budget for emergencies or unexpected expenses. Having a financial cushion can provide peace of mind and prevent financial stress during your trip.

- Local and Affordable Dining: While Mauritius offers fine dining experiences, don't miss out on the chance to savor local street food and affordable eateries. This not only saves money but also allows you to taste authentic Mauritian cuisine.

- Use Public Transportation: Consider using public transportation, such as buses or shared taxis, which is often more budget-friendly than private transfers or rental cars.

By understanding the Mauritian Rupee, managing your finances effectively through credit cards and ATMs, and budgeting according to your preferences, you'll be well-prepared to enjoy your trip to Mauritius without any financial hiccups. Financial planning not only ensures your peace of mind but also enables you to make the most of your travel experience on this stunning island.

# Chapter 2: Navigating Mauritius

Mauritius, a captivating island in the Indian Ocean, offers travelers a diverse range of experiences, from pristine beaches to lush forests and vibrant cities. To make the most of your visit, it's essential to understand how to navigate the island efficiently. This chapter provides valuable insights into getting around Mauritius, exploring the local transportation options, and navigating the linguistic landscape.

## Getting Around the Island

Mauritius is a relatively small island, roughly 2,040 square kilometers in size, but it's packed with attractions spread across different regions. Here, we'll explore the various ways you can get around and explore the island's treasures:

## Renting a Car: Exploring Mauritius at Your Own Pace

One of the most liberating ways to explore the stunning landscapes and diverse attractions of Mauritius is by renting a car. Here, we'll delve deeper into the advantages of renting a car, guide you through the renting procedures, provide insights into road conditions, and offer essential tips for safe driving on the left side of the road.

## Advantages of Renting a Car

- Flexibility: Renting a car offers unparalleled freedom to set your own schedule and itinerary. Whether you want to chase the sunrise on the east coast, explore hidden beaches, or venture into the lush interior, having your own vehicle is the key to flexibility.

- Accessibility: Many of Mauritius' hidden gems, such as secluded beaches, waterfalls, and viewpoints, are not easily accessible by public transportation. With a rental car, you can reach these off-the-beaten-path destinations with ease.

- Cost-Effective: Depending on the length of your stay and the number of people in your group, renting a car can be a cost-effective choice, especially if you plan to explore extensively.

## Renting Procedures

Renting a car in Mauritius is a straightforward process, but there are a few important steps to follow:

- Documentation: Ensure you have your valid driver's license from your home country. If your license is not in English or French, an International Driving Permit (IDP) is recommended.

- Booking in Advance: It's advisable to book your rental car in advance, especially during peak tourist seasons.

Numerous rental agencies operate at the airport and in major tourist areas.

- Age Requirement: Most rental companies require drivers to be at least 21 years old, with a minimum of one year of driving experience. Some agencies may have higher age requirements for certain vehicle categories.

- Insurance: Understand the rental company's insurance policies and consider purchasing additional coverage if necessary.

**Road Conditions**

Mauritius boasts a network of well-maintained roads that make driving a pleasure. However, it's essential to be aware of a few key factors:

- Traffic Rules: Mauritius follows British driving rules, which means you drive on the left-hand side of the road. Roundabouts are common, and priority is given to vehicles already in the roundabout.

- Road Signs: Most road signs are in English and French, making navigation relatively straightforward.

- Road Quality: The main highways are in excellent condition, but some rural roads may have potholes. Drive cautiously, especially during and after heavy rain when roads can become slippery.

- Traffic: While traffic congestion is not a significant issue, be prepared for some busy periods, particularly during rush hours in urban areas.

**Tips for Safe Driving**

Driving in a foreign country can be a unique experience, and Mauritius is no exception. To ensure your safety and the safety of others:

- Stay on the Left: Always drive on the left side of the road, and be mindful when turning or changing lanes.

- Speed Limits: Observe speed limits, which are generally well-marked. In urban areas, the speed limit is often 40-60 km/h (25-37 mph), and on highways, it can range from 80-110 km/h (50-68 mph).

- Seatbelts: Ensure all passengers wear seatbelts at all times, and adhere to child safety seat regulations if traveling with children.

- Alcohol: The legal blood alcohol limit is low in Mauritius (0.08%). It's best to avoid alcohol if you plan to drive.

By adhering to these tips and exercising caution, renting a car in Mauritius can be a rewarding and safe way to explore the island's wonders at your own pace. It's an opportunity to create lasting memories while embracing the freedom of the open road in this enchanting paradise.

# Public Buses in Mauritius: Affordable and Comprehensive Transportation

Mauritius boasts an extensive and well-organized public bus system that is not only a cost-effective means of transportation but also a fantastic way to immerse yourself in the local culture and experience the island from a unique perspective. In this section, we'll delve into the intricacies of Mauritius' public bus system, guiding you through routes, schedules, and tips on how to use it effectively during your visit.

## Understanding the Bus System

- Extensive Coverage: The Mauritius bus network crisscrosses the entire island, reaching most towns, cities, and popular tourist destinations. This extensive coverage means you can rely on buses to access many attractions without the need for a private vehicle.

- Route Diversity: Buses follow various routes, each with its own number and designation. These routes are well-marked, making it relatively easy to identify the right bus for your destination. Some routes run along the coast, while others venture into the interior, offering diverse scenic views.

- Frequent Services: Buses typically operate from early morning until late evening, with frequencies varying based on the route and time of day. Major routes often have buses departing every 20 to 30 minutes during peak hours.

## Using the Bus System

- Bus Stops: To catch a bus, head to the nearest bus stop, which is usually marked with a yellow sign displaying the route numbers and a rough schedule. These stops are scattered throughout cities and towns, making them accessible from most accommodations.

- Fares and Tickets: Bus fares are affordable and often cheaper than alternative transportation options. The fare structure is distance-based, so expect to pay more for longer journeys. You can purchase tickets directly from the driver upon boarding, and it's advisable to carry small denominations of Mauritian rupees for convenience.

- Route Information: If you're unsure about which bus to take, you can ask locals or consult a route map available at major bus terminals, tourist information centers, or online. Some buses also have digital displays indicating the next stop, which can be helpful for tourists.

## Tips for a Smooth Bus Experience

- Plan Ahead: It's a good idea to plan your bus journeys in advance, especially for longer trips or if you have tight schedules. Check the bus schedule for your chosen route, and be at the bus stop a few minutes before the scheduled departure time.

- Language: While English and French are widely understood, bus conductors and fellow passengers may primarily speak Mauritian Creole. Learning a few basic Creole phrases for directions and fare inquiries can be helpful.

- Patience: Bus travel in Mauritius can sometimes be crowded, particularly during rush hours. Be patient and prepared for the possibility of standing during your journey, especially on popular routes.

- Safety: Keep an eye on your belongings, especially in crowded buses. Petty theft is rare, but it's best to take precautions.

Using the public bus system in Mauritius not only saves you money but also provides an opportunity to interact with locals and witness the island's daily life up close. It's a practical and authentic way to explore the island while minimizing your environmental impact, making your trip to Mauritius both economical and culturally enriching.

## Taxis: Your Convenient Mode of Transport

Taxis are a ubiquitous and convenient mode of transportation in Mauritius, particularly in urban areas and popular tourist destinations. They offer a flexible and hassle-free way to navigate the island, making them a preferred choice for many travelers. In this section, we'll delve into the world of Mauritian taxis, helping you make the most of this transportation option.

## Availability and Accessibility

Taxis can be found at various points throughout urban areas, near hotels, shopping centers, and major attractions. In cities like Port Louis, Grand Baie, and Flic-en-Flac, you'll have no trouble flagging one down. Most taxi drivers are friendly and accustomed to assisting tourists, so don't hesitate to approach them.

## Short Trips and Day Tours

Taxis in Mauritius can be hired for both short trips within a town or for day tours to explore different parts of the island. Here's what you need to know about each:

- Short Trips: For quick and convenient transportation within a town or from your accommodation to a nearby restaurant or attraction, taxis are ideal. They offer a door-to-door service that saves you time and effort.

- Day Tours: Taxis can also be chartered for day tours, allowing you to explore multiple attractions in a single day. Whether you want to visit the bustling markets of Port Louis, hike to a breathtaking waterfall, or tour historic sites, your taxi driver can customize an itinerary to suit your interests.

**Negotiating Fares**

Negotiating fares with taxi drivers in Mauritius is common practice, especially for longer trips or day tours. Here are some tips for successful fare negotiation:

- Agree on the Price in Advance: Before starting your journey, it's advisable to agree on the fare with the driver. While some taxis have meters, it's a good practice to set a fixed price for your destination or tour to avoid any surprises.

- Ask Locals for Fare Estimates: To ensure you're getting a fair rate, consider asking locals or your hotel staff for an estimated fare for your journey. This can serve as a reference point during negotiations.

- Be Polite and Respectful: Politeness goes a long way when negotiating fares. Maintain a friendly and respectful demeanor, even if negotiations become heated. A smile and some basic Creole phrases can help build rapport.

- Consider the Distance and Time: Fares may vary depending on the distance you're traveling and the time of day. Longer journeys or late-night rides may cost more.

**Ensuring a Comfortable Ride**

To ensure a comfortable and safe ride, keep these considerations in mind:

- Vehicle Condition: Before entering the taxi, take a moment to assess its condition. Ensure the vehicle is in good repair and that seatbelts are available and functional.

- Driver Identification: Many taxis in Mauritius display their driver's identification prominently. Make a mental note of the driver's name and license number for added security.

- Communication: If you have specific requests or need assistance during your journey, don't hesitate to communicate with your driver. Most taxi drivers in Mauritius are knowledgeable about the island and can offer valuable insights.

In conclusion, taxis in Mauritius are a reliable and flexible transportation option for getting around the island. By understanding how to negotiate fares and ensuring a comfortable ride, you'll make the most of your taxi experience, allowing you to explore Mauritius with ease and convenience.

## Cycling in Mauritius: Embracing Eco-Friendly Exploration

Cycling in Mauritius offers a unique and eco-friendly way to explore this tropical paradise. With its lush landscapes, stunning coastlines, and picturesque villages, the island is a cycling enthusiast's dream. In this section, we'll delve into the world of cycling on the island, providing you with insights into why it's such a fantastic option, where to find the best scenic routes, and how to access bike rental services.

## Why Choose Cycling?

- Eco-Friendly: Mauritius is committed to sustainability and preserving its natural beauty. Cycling is an eco-friendly mode of transportation that aligns perfectly with the island's green ethos. As you pedal through scenic routes, you'll reduce your carbon footprint and contribute to the preservation of this pristine environment.

- Immersive Experience: Cycling allows you to experience Mauritius at a pace that lets you savor every moment. You can stop whenever you please to take in breathtaking views, interact with locals, and discover hidden gems that may be missed when using other modes of transport.

- Health and Well-Being: Cycling is not only a great way to explore; it's also an excellent form of exercise. It's a chance to stay active, soak up the island's positive energy, and maintain your well-being while on vacation.

## Scenic Routes

Mauritius boasts a wide range of scenic cycling routes that cater to all skill levels. Here are some of the must-ride routes:

- Coastal Beauty: The coastal road from Belle Mare to Le Morne offers stunning sea views. You'll pass by pristine beaches, fishing villages, and charming coastal towns.

- Tea Plantation Trail: Explore the lush, rolling hills of the Bois Chéri tea plantation. This route combines natural beauty with cultural insights into Mauritius' tea-making heritage.

- The Heart of the Island: Cycle through the picturesque villages of the interior, such as Curepipe and Moka. These routes offer a glimpse into the authentic Mauritian way of life.

- Black River Gorges National Park: For more adventurous cyclists, the park offers challenging terrain and the chance to encounter Mauritius' unique flora and fauna.

- Northern Coastline: From Grand Baie to Cap Malheureux, this route treats you to scenic beaches, bustling markets, and the iconic red-roofed church.

**Bike Rental Services**

To make your cycling adventure a reality, you'll need access to quality bicycles. Fortunately, Mauritius has a growing number of bike rental services, especially in tourist areas like Grand Baie and Flic en Flac. Here's what you should know:

- Types of Bicycles: Rental shops typically offer a range of bicycles, including mountain bikes, road bikes, and hybrid bikes. Choose one that suits your preferred riding style and the terrain you plan to explore.

- Rates and Durations: Rental rates vary, but they are generally reasonable. You can rent a bike for a few hours or several days, depending on your itinerary.

- Safety Gear: Rental shops often provide helmets, locks, and other safety gear. Don't forget to ask for these essentials to ensure a safe and enjoyable ride.

- Reservations: It's a good idea to reserve your bike in advance, especially during peak tourist seasons.

Cycling in Mauritius is not just a means of transportation; it's an adventure in itself. Whether you're a leisure cyclist or a hardcore enthusiast, the island has something to offer everyone. So, gear up, hop on your bike, and get ready to explore Mauritius in an eco-friendly and unforgettable way.

## Walking Tours: Exploring Port Louis and Grand Baie on Foot

Walking tours offer a unique and immersive way to experience the cultural richness and vibrant atmosphere of Mauritius. In this section, we'll delve into why some areas, specifically Port Louis and Grand Baie, are best explored on foot and provide insights into guided walking tours and self-guided routes.

**Port Louis: A Step Back in Time**

Port Louis, the capital city of Mauritius, is a treasure trove of history, culture, and architecture. Its compact size and bustling streets make it ideal for exploring on foot. Here's what you can expect:

- Historical Sites: Port Louis boasts a fascinating history influenced by Dutch, French, and British colonial periods. Walking through the city's streets allows you to discover historic landmarks such as Fort Adelaide, the Aapravasi Ghat (a UNESCO World Heritage Site), and the Jummah Mosque.

- Local Markets: Dive into the heart of Mauritian culture by visiting the bustling Central Market (Bazar Port Louis) and the nearby Chinatown market. These vibrant markets offer a sensory overload of sights, sounds, and tastes.

- Street Food Delights: Savor local street food like dholl puri, farata, and gateau piment from street vendors. We'll provide recommendations on where to find the best bites.

- Shopping Opportunities: Explore the charming streets lined with shops selling everything from clothing and handicrafts to souvenirs. Discover unique items and support local artisans.

**Grand Baie: Coastal Charm and Shopping Galore**

Grand Baie, located on the northern coast of Mauritius, is renowned for its stunning beaches, vibrant nightlife, and shopping opportunities. Here's why a walking tour in this area is a must:

- Beachfront Strolls: Take leisurely walks along the beautiful Grand Baie Beach and enjoy the crystal-clear waters and picturesque sunsets.

- Waterfront Dining: Discover an array of restaurants and cafes with stunning views of the bay. We'll recommend some of the best spots to savor seafood and international cuisine.

- Shopping District: Grand Baie is a shopper's paradise. Explore the vibrant shopping districts, including Sunset Boulevard and La Croisette Shopping Complex, where you can find designer boutiques, local crafts, and duty-free goods.

- Nightlife: Experience the lively nightlife scene with bars, clubs, and live music venues. We'll provide suggestions for enjoying the after-hours entertainment.

**Guided Walking Tours vs. Self-Guided Exploration**

Now that you're intrigued by the idea of walking tours in Port Louis and Grand Baie, you have two main options:

- Guided Walking Tours: Consider joining a guided walking tour led by knowledgeable local guides. These tours often provide historical context, insider insights, and access to places you might not discover on your own. You'll also have the chance to ask questions and interact with fellow travelers.

- Self-Guided Exploration: If you prefer a more independent experience, we'll offer self-guided walking routes with detailed maps, points of interest, and recommendations for where to stop along the way. This option allows you to explore at your own pace and personalize your itinerary.

Whichever option you choose, walking tours in Port Louis and Grand Baie promise an immersive journey into the heart of Mauritius, where you can connect with the local culture, history, and natural beauty on a more intimate level.

## Language and Communication

Mauritius boasts a rich linguistic diversity reflective of its multicultural heritage. Understanding the local languages and communication norms enhances your travel experience:

### Official Languages: English and French

In the colorful tapestry of languages spoken on the island of Mauritius, English and French stand as the official languages, remnants of its colonial past. Understanding the role of these languages in Mauritius is not only a practical necessity for travelers but also an intriguing glimpse into the island's history and culture.

**English in Mauritius:**

English, a legacy of British colonial rule (1810-1968), holds a significant place in the educational and administrative spheres. In fact, it is the medium of instruction in schools and is widely used in government proceedings. While most Mauritians are fluent in English, it may not be their first language for everyday conversation. Nonetheless, you'll find that English is widely understood, especially in urban areas and tourist destinations.

**French in Mauritius:**

French, a testament to the island's period of French colonization (1715-1810), is another official language of Mauritius. Although it's not as dominant in everyday life as English, it still plays a significant role. French is often used in legal documents, and many Mauritians receive their education in French. It's worth noting that the French spoken in Mauritius has a distinct local flavor, influenced by Creole and other languages.

**Mauritian Creole: The Heartbeat of Communication**

While English and French are the official languages, the true heartbeat of Mauritian communication is Mauritian Creole (often simply referred to as "Creole"). Creole is a rich, expressive language with influences from French, African languages, Hindi, and more. It's the language of the home, the marketplace, and the street. Understanding a bit of Creole can truly enhance your interactions with locals and provide a deeper insight into the culture. Here are some basic phrases and etiquette tips:

Basic Creole Phrases:

- Bonjour - Good morning
- Bonswar - Good evening
- Ki manyer? - How are you?
- Mo kontan rankont twa. - Nice to meet you.
- Kuma ou appel? - What is your name?
- Kombien sa koute? - How much does this cost?
- Dimer ki sa? - What is this?
- Mersi - Thank you
- Si ou plé - Please
- Sakenn - Everyone

**Etiquette Tips:**

- Greet with a Smile: A friendly smile goes a long way in Mauritius. When approaching someone, whether for a question or just to say hello, a warm smile is a sign of respect.

- Use Simple Creole Phrases: While many Mauritians are proficient in English and French, attempting a few words in Creole is greatly appreciated. It shows that you respect and are interested in their culture.

- Respectful Gestures: Handshakes are common in Mauritius as a sign of greeting. However, in more informal settings, like among friends or in markets, cheek-kissing (air kisses) may also be used.

**Signage and Navigation**

When navigating the streets and roads of Mauritius, you'll encounter a mix of languages on signs, including English, French, and sometimes Creole. Here's how to navigate effectively:

1. Road Signs:

- Directional Signs: These are typically in English and French and are easy to understand for travelers. For instance, "Port Louis" in English and "Port-Louis" in French both lead to the capital city.
- Hazard Signs: Warning signs, such as those indicating curves, intersections, and pedestrian crossings, are usually in both English and French with universally recognized symbols.
- Place Names: Names of towns and landmarks are often bilingual, like "Grand Baie" and "Grande Baie" (English and French versions of the same place).

2. Public Information:

- Government Buildings: Official information from government offices is primarily in English and French.

- Tourist Information: In tourist-heavy areas, you'll find signage, brochures, and maps in multiple languages, including English and French, to cater to international visitors.

## Communication Challenges

While language barriers are generally minimal in Mauritius due to the prevalence of English and French, there can still be some challenges, especially in more remote or less touristy areas. Here's how to navigate these challenges and communicate effectively:

1. Multilingualism: Mauritians often switch between languages in conversations, seamlessly blending English, French, and Creole. Don't be surprised if you hear a mix in everyday interactions.

2. Language Variations: Keep in mind that French spoken in Mauritius has a local accent and may differ slightly from the standard French taught in textbooks. Similarly, Creole has many regional variations.

3. Patience and Courtesy: If you encounter someone who doesn't speak your language fluently, patience and a friendly demeanor can go a long way. Try simple words, gestures, and a smile to bridge the gap.

4. Translation Apps: Consider using translation apps on your smartphone to help with more complex or specific communication needs.

In summary, while English and French serve as the official languages in Mauritius, Mauritian Creole is the heart and soul of everyday communication. Understanding the linguistic landscape of the island, along with some basic Creole phrases, not only aids practical communication but also enriches your cultural experience as you engage with the warm and welcoming people of Mauritius.

# Chapter 3: Island Regions and Their Charms

Mauritius is a diverse and captivating island nation, offering a wide range of experiences across its various regions. In this chapter, we will explore the unique charms of four distinct areas: Port Louis, Grand Baie, Mahebourg, and the tranquil Rodrigues Island.

## Exploring Port Louis: The Capital City

Port Louis, the lively and dynamic capital of Mauritius, is a microcosm of the island's rich history, vibrant culture, and economic prowess. Nestled along the northwest coast of the island, this bustling city is a must-visit destination for travelers seeking to uncover the heart and soul of Mauritius. In this section, we embark on a journey through Port Louis, where we'll delve into the captivating facets that make it an essential stop on any Mauritius itinerary.

**Historic Quarters: Tracing the Colonial Tapestry**

As you step into Port Louis, it's like taking a step back in time to a colonial era where diverse influences shaped the cityscape. The historic quarters of Port Louis are a testament to its rich colonial history:

Chinatown: Begin your exploration in the lively streets of Chinatown, where the vibrant colors, aromatic street food, and bustling markets transport you to a different world. This neighborhood, with its fusion of Chinese, Indian, and Mauritian cultures, exemplifies the island's diversity.

French Colonial Buildings: The city is dotted with charming French colonial buildings, each telling a story of the island's colonial past. Stroll along the cobblestone streets and admire the architectural marvels like the Government House and the old theater, the Theatre Royal.

Fort Adelaide (La Citadelle): For panoramic views of the city and its surroundings, ascend to Fort Adelaide, locally known as La Citadelle. This historical fortress offers not only a glimpse into the past but also an opportunity to appreciate the modern city's layout.

**Central Market: A Feast for the Senses**

One of the highlights of a visit to Port Louis is undoubtedly the Central Market. This bustling bazaar is a sensory paradise where you can immerse yourself in the vibrant culture and flavors of Mauritius:

Exotic Spices: As you enter the market, you'll be greeted by the heady aroma of exotic spices that permeates the air. Traders peddle spices like cinnamon, saffron, and vanilla, which are essential ingredients in Mauritian cuisine. Don't hesitate to engage with the vendors, who are often eager to share their knowledge.

Fresh Produce: Rows of colorful stalls showcase a bounty of tropical fruits and vegetables, from lychees and mangoes to chayote and breadfruit. Take the opportunity to taste local varieties you may not find anywhere else.

Street Food Delights: The Central Market is a paradise for food enthusiasts. Local vendors dish out delectable street food like dholl puri (stuffed lentil flatbread), gateau piment (chili cakes), and alouda (a sweet, pink milk drink). These authentic flavors are a true reflection of the island's multicultural culinary heritage.

## Caudan Waterfront: The Modern Face of Port Louis

A short stroll from the historic quarters brings you to the Caudan Waterfront, a symbol of the modernization and transformation of Port Louis. Here, you'll find a juxtaposition of contemporary amenities with a touch of heritage:

Shopping Extravaganza: The Caudan Waterfront is a shopping haven, boasting a wide range of boutiques, brand-name stores, and artisan shops. Whether you're looking for designer fashion, local crafts, or souvenirs, you'll find it here.

Gourmet Dining: The waterfront area offers an array of dining options, from local seafood restaurants to international cuisines. Savor the catch of the day while enjoying scenic views of the harbor.

Cultural Attractions: Cultural enthusiasts will appreciate the Blue Penny Museum, home to one of the world's rarest stamps, and the Photography Museum. Both provide insights into the history and culture of Mauritius.

## Aapravasi Ghat: A UNESCO World Heritage Site

Delve deeper into Port Louis's historical significance by visiting the Aapravasi Ghat, a UNESCO World Heritage-listed site. This poignant place, steeped in history, tells the story of indentured laborers who arrived on the island:

Historical Significance: The Aapravasi Ghat was the first immigration depot in Mauritius, serving as the gateway for indentured laborers arriving from India and other parts of the world. It played a pivotal role in shaping the island's cultural and demographic landscape.

Cultural Significance: This site is not only a reminder of the island's complex history but also a tribute to the resilience and contributions of the laborers and their descendants. It stands as a symbol of unity and diversity in Mauritius.

The Museum: Explore the museum on-site, which provides a comprehensive understanding of the indenture system, the living conditions of the laborers, and the cultural exchanges that took place.

As you wander through Port Louis, it becomes evident that the city is a captivating blend of the old and the new, where history and modernity coexist harmoniously. Its rich colonial heritage, vibrant markets, and cultural landmarks make it an essential stop for any traveler seeking to unravel the captivating tapestry of Mauritius. Port Louis, with its diverse influences and historical significance, is indeed a testament to the island's unique identity and enduring charm.

# Grand Baie: A Hub of Entertainment and Shopping

Nestled on the northern coast of Mauritius, Grand Baie stands as a vibrant testament to the island's fusion of natural beauty and cosmopolitan charm. It's no wonder that this coastal town has earned its reputation as one of Mauritius's premier destinations for travelers seeking a blend of relaxation, adventure, and entertainment. In this section, we'll embark on a journey to uncover the multifaceted allure of Grand Baie.

**Beaches and Water Sports**

The beaches of Grand Baie are undoubtedly among the most enticing on the island. Powdery white sands meet the turquoise embrace of the Indian Ocean, creating a picture-perfect setting for visitors to bask in the sun's warm caress.

One of the crown jewels of Grand Baie is undoubtedly La Cuvette Beach. Tucked away from the bustling town center, this serene cove offers a tranquil escape for those looking to unwind. Sunbathing here becomes an art form, as the gentle lapping of waves provides a soothing background score.

For those seeking adventure on the water, Grand Baie offers a smorgasbord of aquatic activities. Snorkeling is a must-do, as the coral reefs surrounding the area teem with vibrant marine life. Grab your mask and fins to explore an underwater world of technicolor fish and intricate corals.

Parasailing is another exhilarating way to take in the coastal vistas from a unique perspective. As you ascend into the skies, the panoramic views of the coastline, dotted with luxurious resorts and lush greenery, are nothing short of breathtaking.

**Shopping Paradise**

Grand Baie is more than just a beach destination; it's a shopper's paradise. From luxury boutiques to quaint craft shops and bustling markets, this town offers a treasure trove of retail therapy options.

The Grand Baie Bazaar is a bustling market where you can immerse yourself in the vibrant colors and scents of Mauritius. Stalls here showcase local craftsmanship, from intricately woven textiles to handmade jewelry. Don't forget to bargain a bit – it's all part of the experience!

For high-end fashion and designer brands, Sunset Boulevard is the place to be. Here, you can browse a range of boutiques that cater to every fashionista's whim. Whether you're in search of a stylish swimsuit or the perfect beach cover-up, you'll find it here.

Art enthusiasts will appreciate the offerings of Art 18 gallery, where you can peruse contemporary and traditional Mauritian art. Local artists frequently exhibit their work here, giving you a glimpse into the island's creative spirit.

## Nightlife and Entertainment

As the sun dips below the horizon, Grand Baie transforms into a buzzing nightlife hub. The town's bars, clubs, and restaurants offer a diverse range of evening entertainment options.

Banana Beach Club is a beachfront hotspot where you can sip on tropical cocktails while listening to live music or DJ sets. The laid-back atmosphere is perfect for mingling with fellow travelers.

For those who enjoy a bit of gaming excitement, the Grand Baie Casino beckons with its slot machines, card tables, and roulette wheels. It's a place where luck and strategy dance hand in hand.

La Croisette is a modern shopping and entertainment complex that features a cinema, restaurants, and even a bowling alley. It's a great place for a family outing or a casual evening with friends.

As the night progresses, the town's restaurants come alive. From sumptuous seafood grills at La Rougaille Creole to international cuisine at Le Capitaine, there's a culinary adventure awaiting every palate.

For those who crave the dance floor, Les Enfants Terribles and Insomnia are among the popular nightclubs where you can groove to the beats of local and international DJs.

In addition to its nightlife, Grand Baie often hosts cultural events and festivals, so be sure to check the local calendar for any exciting happenings during your visit.

In conclusion, Grand Baie encapsulates the essence of Mauritius's northern coast. With its stunning beaches, vibrant water sports scene, diverse shopping opportunities, and lively nightlife, it's a destination that promises a well-rounded and unforgettable vacation experience. Whether you're seeking relaxation, adventure, or a bit of both, Grand Baie has something to offer every traveler.

## Cultural Treasures of Mahebourg

In the quiet and unassuming town of Mahebourg, nestled along the southeastern coast of the enchanting island of Mauritius, lies a treasure trove of culture, history, and culinary delights waiting to be discovered. Often overshadowed by the island's more famous attractions, Mahebourg holds within its charming streets a wealth of cultural riches that offer visitors a profound glimpse into the essence of this tropical paradise.

**The Naval Museum: Unraveling Mauritius' Maritime Legacy**

As you step into the Naval Museum of Mahebourg, you embark on a journey through time, one that unravels the maritime tapestry of Mauritius. This museum is a living testament to the island's historical significance as a maritime hub and a pivotal location during the colonial era.

The museum's collection is a treasure trove of artifacts, each with a story to tell. Model ships from various eras grace the exhibit halls, offering insights into the evolution of naval craftsmanship. You can't help but be captivated by the sight of centuries-old cannons that once guarded these shores. These silent sentinels bear witness to countless maritime battles and the ebb and flow of Mauritian history.

The true gems of the museum, however, are the shipwrecks. As you stand before these remnants of vessels that met their fate off the treacherous shores of Mauritius, you can almost hear the creaking of the timbers and the shouts of sailors long gone. The HMS Sirius, a British frigate lost during the Napoleonic Wars, takes center stage, its preserved timbers a poignant reminder of a bygone era.

The museum's exhibits don't just showcase the grandeur of naval warfare; they also delve into the everyday lives of sailors and the cultural exchanges that occurred between the island and the world. Maps, navigational instruments, and personal items from sailors offer a glimpse into the human stories behind the maritime history.

But it's not just the artifacts that make this museum special. It's the passionate guides who breathe life into these exhibits, sharing tales of the sea, the battles, and the island's resilience. Their narratives bring history to life, making a visit here more than just a museum tour – it's an immersion into Mauritius' seafaring soul.

## Mahebourg Waterfront: Where Time Meets the Sea

After an enriching visit to the Naval Museum, take a leisurely stroll along the picturesque Mahebourg Waterfront. This is where time seems to slow down, and the rhythmic lapping of the waves against the shore becomes the soundtrack to your journey.

As you amble along the waterfront promenade, you'll be greeted by a panorama of blues – the azure sea stretching to the horizon, the cobalt sky meeting the tranquil waters. Seabirds glide gracefully overhead, adding to the sense of serenity that envelopes this place.

Local fishermen can often be seen mending their nets or casting their lines from the old wooden jetties that dot the waterfront. Their presence is a reminder of Mahebourg's enduring connection to the sea. Conversations with them may unveil tales of the day's catch, and perhaps even secrets of the best fishing spots.

The charm of Mahebourg is not just in its natural beauty but in its blend of past and present. Along the waterfront, you'll find charming Creole houses with their wooden balconies and vibrant colors, a testament to the island's architectural heritage. These houses have witnessed centuries of history and change, yet they remain steadfast, like guardians of Mahebourg's soul.

As you explore the town's streets branching off from the waterfront, you'll discover local shops and boutiques selling crafts, clothing, and souvenirs. The Bazar Couleur

Mahebourg is a particularly lively spot, offering an array of handmade items that reflect the vibrant culture of Mauritius.

Perhaps one of the most enchanting moments along the waterfront occurs during sunset. As the sun dips below the horizon, casting a warm, golden glow across the sea, you'll witness a breathtaking spectacle. The sky ignites with hues of orange and pink, and the tranquil waters shimmer with the last light of day. It's a time for quiet reflection, a moment to absorb the natural beauty of Mahebourg and the profound connection between this town and the sea.

**Local Cuisine: Savoring the Flavors of Mauritius**

No cultural exploration is complete without indulging in the local cuisine, and Mahebourg is a gastronomic treasure trove waiting to be explored. The town's culinary scene is a reflection of Mauritius' diverse heritage, blending flavors from India, China, Africa, and Europe into a unique culinary tapestry.

Mahebourg's streets come alive with the enticing aromas of Mauritian cuisine. Follow your nose to the Marché de Mahebourg, a bustling market where vendors peddle fresh produce, aromatic spices, and local delicacies. It's a sensory delight, a place where you can witness the raw ingredients that go into creating the island's flavorful dishes.

To truly savor the essence of Mauritian cuisine, you must dine at the local eateries and street food stalls that line the streets of Mahebourg. Here, you can indulge in traditional dishes that have been passed down through generations, each bite a symphony of flavors.

Start your culinary adventure with a steaming bowl of dholl puri, a type of flatbread stuffed with spiced yellow split peas, often served with a side of chutney and pickles. It's a popular street food item, and the blend of textures and flavors is a testament to the Indian influence on Mauritian cuisine.

Another must-try is rougaille, a tomato-based sauce that serves as the foundation for a variety of dishes. It can be paired with fish, chicken, or sausages, and its rich, tangy taste is a taste of the island's Creole heritage.

For seafood enthusiasts, Mahebourg is a paradise. Freshly caught fish and prawns are transformed into delectable dishes, such as cari poisson (fish curry) and camarons grillé (grilled prawns). The seafood is often marinated in a mixture of local spices and cooked to perfection, resulting in dishes that burst with flavor.

As you dine in the town's small restaurants or at street food stalls, don't be surprised if the chef invites you into the kitchen. This is a common practice in Mauritius, a sign of the warmth and hospitality that defines the island's culture. It's a chance to witness the culinary magic as dishes are prepared with love and precision.

To complement your meal, be sure to try a refreshing glass of alouda, a sweet and creamy drink made from agar-agar, milk, and flavored syrups. It's the perfect accompaniment to spicy Mauritian dishes, offering a delightful contrast.

Dining in Mahebourg is not just about satisfying your taste buds; it's about immersing yourself in the island's culture, where food is a celebration of heritage and a reflection of the warm hospitality of the Mauritian people.

In Mahebourg, history, natural beauty, and culinary traditions come together to create a rich tapestry of culture. It's a town where the echoes of the past can be heard in the stories of the sea, where the present is a harmonious blend of tradition and modernity, and where the flavors of Mauritius come alive in every dish. Mahebourg may be small in size, but its cultural treasures are boundless, offering visitors an opportunity to connect with the heart and soul of this extraordinary island.

## Tranquility of Rodrigues Island

Nestled in the azure embrace of the Indian Ocean, Rodrigues Island, an autonomous outer island of Mauritius, is an oasis of tranquility and natural beauty. This remote gem offers a serene and unspoiled escape from the bustling mainland, making it a destination that beckons travelers seeking solace in nature's embrace.

**Getting to Rodrigues**

Embarking on a journey to Rodrigues is an adventure in itself. To reach this secluded paradise, travelers typically take a short flight from Sir Seewoosagur Ramgoolam International Airport in Mauritius to Sir Gaëtan Duval

Airport on Rodrigues. Several airlines operate regular flights, making it relatively easy to access this island haven.

Upon arrival at Sir Gaëtan Duval Airport, you'll instantly notice the change in pace. The airport itself is a testament to the island's modesty, with its welcoming staff and unhurried atmosphere. From the airport, you can arrange transportation to your accommodation, which might include quaint guesthouses, cozy cottages, or charming beachfront resorts, each offering a unique perspective of Rodriguan hospitality.

As you settle into Rodrigues, you'll find that the absence of large crowds and the presence of warm, welcoming locals set the tone for a truly relaxed and rejuvenating escape.

**Natural Beauty**

Rodrigues Island is a masterpiece of nature, where time seems to slow down, allowing you to immerse yourself in its pristine landscapes and awe-inspiring vistas.

Secluded Beaches: The island is renowned for its untouched beaches, often secluded and flanked by swaying palm trees. Whether you seek solitude or a romantic spot to watch the sunrise, these beaches offer the perfect backdrop.

Coral Reefs and Marine Life: Beneath the crystalline waters surrounding Rodrigues lies a mesmerizing world of coral reefs teeming with marine life. Snorkeling and diving enthusiasts can explore these vibrant ecosystems, encountering colorful fish, sea turtles, and even dolphins if fortune favors.

Scenic Hiking Trails: If you're an adventure seeker, Rodrigues offers a network of hiking trails that wind through its undulating terrain. As you ascend the island's gentle hills, you'll be treated to breathtaking panoramas of the coastline and interior. Trails like Mont Limon and Trou d'Argent are favorites among hikers, each offering a unique perspective of Rodrigues' natural beauty.

Birdwatching in Rodrigues: The island is a haven for birdwatchers, with several endemic species to spot, including the Rodrigues Fody and the Rodrigues Warbler. These feathered residents can be observed in their natural habitat, providing bird enthusiasts with a rare and rewarding experience.

**Cultural Experiences**

Beyond its natural splendor, Rodrigues Island boasts a rich cultural heritage, shaped by centuries of isolation and traditions passed down through generations. Exploring the island's cultural tapestry is a delightful journey into the heart of Rodrigues.

Traditional Music and Dance: Rodriguan culture comes alive through traditional music and dance performances. Local musicians play instruments like the ravanne and triangle, creating infectious rhythms that beckon you to join in the dance. The Sega, a traditional dance, is a vibrant expression of the island's heritage, characterized by swaying hips and colorful costumes.

Culinary Adventures: A visit to Rodrigues wouldn't be complete without savoring its unique cuisine. Creole flavors dominate the local dishes, with staples like octopus curry, fried rice, and fresh seafood gracing menus. Don't miss the chance to dine at family-run restaurants or enjoy a home-cooked meal with locals.

Cultural Events and Festivals: Throughout the year, Rodrigues hosts a range of cultural events and festivals that showcase its vibrant heritage. The Festival International Kreol is a highlight, celebrating Creole culture through music, dance, and traditional food. Rodriguans take immense pride in sharing their culture with visitors, and you'll find a warm welcome at these events.

Crafts and Souvenirs: Rodrigues is known for its artisanal crafts, including woven baskets, hats, and jewelry made from locally sourced materials. Visiting craft markets provides an opportunity to support local artisans and take home a piece of Rodriguan culture.

Rodrigues Island is a haven for those seeking respite from the hectic pace of modern life. Its accessibility, combined with its untouched natural beauty and rich cultural heritage, make it a destination that offers a truly transformative travel experience. Whether you're exploring the island's pristine beaches, diving into its coral reefs, or immersing yourself in its vibrant culture, Rodrigues is a place where you can reconnect with nature and find inner peace.

# Chamarel and the Southwest Coast

Nestled in the southwestern part of the enchanting island of Mauritius, the region of Chamarel beckons travelers with its unparalleled natural beauty and a wealth of attractions that showcase the island's geological, cultural, and natural diversity. Chamarel is an integral part of any Mauritius travel itinerary, and in this section, we will embark on a journey to explore its captivating charms.

**Seven Colored Earths: A Geological Marvel**

One of the most captivating natural wonders that Chamarel proudly boasts is the "Seven Colored Earths." This geological phenomenon is a testament to nature's artistic prowess, where sands of seven distinct colors - red, brown, violet, blue, green, and yellow - converge to create a surreal and visually stunning landscape.

As you stand before this remarkable tableau, you'll be awestruck by the vibrancy of the colors, which seem almost otherworldly. The colors are not merely surface-deep; they extend to depths of up to 15 meters, making this phenomenon even more mystifying. Over the years, scientists have attributed these varying hues to the varying mineral compositions in the sands.

The site is thoughtfully preserved, allowing visitors to explore the Seven Colored Earths via well-maintained pathways and observation points. The best time to visit is during the morning or late afternoon when the sunlight enhances the brilliance of the colors. It's a place where you can not only witness the wonders of nature but also contemplate the mysteries of our planet's geology.

## Chamarel Waterfall: Nature's Masterpiece

Adjacent to the Seven Colored Earths lies another natural gem, the majestic Chamarel Waterfall. Plunging from a height of approximately 100 meters, it's one of the highest waterfalls in Mauritius. The waterfall's name originates from the village of Chamarel, and it's often referred to as the "Cascade de Chamarel."

To reach this enchanting site, you'll venture through lush tropical vegetation, where the air is filled with the soothing sounds of nature. As you approach the waterfall, the spray of mist in the air is invigorating, and the sight of the water cascading down the rocky cliffs is nothing short of breathtaking.

Many visitors choose to take a leisurely stroll to the viewing platform, which provides a panoramic view of the waterfall and its surroundings. For the more adventurous, there are hiking trails that lead to the base of the waterfall, where you can feel the cool spray on your skin and witness the sheer power of nature up close.

The Chamarel Waterfall is not only a sight to behold but also a place of tranquility and reflection. It's a reminder of the untamed beauty that lies at the heart of Mauritius, a paradise where nature reigns supreme.

## Rhumerie de Chamarel: A Journey into Rum-Making

Just a stone's throw away from the Seven Colored Earths and Chamarel Waterfall is the Rhumerie de Chamarel, a place where the art of rum-making is celebrated with passion and expertise. This distillery is a testament to the historical significance of sugarcane and rum production in Mauritius.

Upon arrival at the Rhumerie de Chamarel, you'll be welcomed into a world of sensory delights. The lush sugarcane fields that surround the distillery provide a serene backdrop, setting the stage for an immersive journey into the world of rum.

A guided tour of the distillery takes you through the entire rum-making process, from the harvesting of sugarcane to the distillation and aging of the spirits. Knowledgeable guides share the history and intricacies of rum production in Mauritius, offering a deep insight into the island's cultural heritage.

The highlight of the tour is undoubtedly the tasting session. Here, you have the opportunity to sample a range of rum flavors, each with its own distinct character and complexity. From light and fruity to rich and smoky, the Rhumerie de Chamarel offers a diverse palette of tastes to explore.

To complement your rum tasting experience, the distillery also houses a delightful restaurant. Here, you can savor a delicious meal featuring local ingredients and flavors, all while overlooking the picturesque sugarcane fields.

## Black River Gorges National Park: A Biodiversity Hotspot

Beyond the geological wonders of Chamarel, the region also encompasses the sprawling expanse of the Black River Gorges National Park. This national park is a testament to Mauritius' commitment to preserving its natural heritage and is a sanctuary for rare bird species, unique flora, and outdoor enthusiasts.

The park is a haven for hikers, with a network of well-maintained trails that traverse its lush terrain. The most famous trail is the Black River Peak Trail, which culminates at the island's highest point, offering panoramic views of the surrounding landscapes.

As you hike through the park's dense forests, you'll encounter a wealth of endemic plant species, including rare orchids and the iconic dodo tree, named after the infamous flightless bird that once inhabited the island. Birdwatchers will be delighted by the opportunity to spot indigenous avian species, including the colorful Mauritian kestrel and echo parakeet.

The Black River Gorges National Park is a vital conservation area, protecting the island's natural heritage and providing a glimpse into the pristine ecosystems that once covered Mauritius. It's a place where nature enthusiasts and adventure seekers can come together to appreciate the island's rich biodiversity.

In conclusion, Chamarel and the southwestern region of Mauritius are a treasure trove of natural wonders, cultural richness, and outdoor adventures. From the mesmerizing Seven Colored Earths to the tranquil beauty of Chamarel Waterfall, the immersive experience at Rhumerie de Chamarel, and the biodiversity of Black River Gorges National Park, this region embodies the essence of Mauritius. It's a place where the past and present coexist harmoniously, inviting travelers to explore the diverse charms of the island and forge lasting memories of their visit.

# Flic-en-Flac and the West Coast

Nestled along the western shoreline of the enchanting island of Mauritius, Flic-en-Flac stands as a testament to the island's enduring allure as a beachfront haven. As you venture into this captivating region, you'll discover that Flic-en-Flac is not just another beach destination; it's a tropical paradise characterized by its laid-back vibe, stunning sunsets, and a plethora of attractions that beckon to the adventurer and the relaxation seeker alike.

### Beach Bliss: Flic-en-Flac's Golden Shores

The crowning jewel of Flic-en-Flac is undoubtedly its pristine beach, aptly named Flic-en-Flac Beach. This expanse of golden sands stretches for kilometers along the coastline, offering a sanctuary of serenity for beachgoers. What sets this beach apart is not just its beauty, but also its calm, crystal-clear waters, which make it an ideal spot for swimming and sunbathing.

As you set foot on the soft sands of Flic-en-Flac Beach, you'll immediately be struck by the sense of tranquility that envelops you. The gentle lapping of the waves against the shore provides a soothing soundtrack to your day of relaxation. Whether you're lounging under the shade of a palm tree with a good book in hand or taking a leisurely stroll along the water's edge, the beach beckons you to embrace the moment, leaving your cares behind.

What truly sets Flic-en-Flac Beach apart is its accessibility. Unlike some of the more remote beaches on the island, Flic-en-Flac is easily reached from major towns and resorts, making it a popular choice for both locals and tourists. Whether you're a seasoned traveler or a first-time visitor to Mauritius, the allure of Flic-en-Flac Beach is undeniable.

**Dolphin Watching: A Glimpse into Marine Magic**

Just a stone's throw away from Flic-en-Flac lies Tamarin Bay, a renowned hotspot for dolphin watching. Here, you can embark on a thrilling aquatic adventure as you set sail in search of these playful marine mammals in their natural habitat.

Mauritius is home to several species of dolphins, and Tamarin Bay offers one of the best opportunities to observe them up close. As your boat glides through the turquoise waters, keep your eyes peeled for the telltale signs of dolphin activity - the joyful leaps, playful flips, and occasional dorsal fins breaking the surface.

The experience of encountering dolphins in their natural environment is nothing short of magical. These intelligent creatures often swim alongside the boats, seemingly as curious about you as you are about them. It's a humbling and awe-inspiring moment that reminds you of the beauty and wonder of the natural world.

Dolphin watching tours from Flic-en-Flac are typically led by experienced guides who prioritize the well-being and conservation of these marine species. They provide valuable insights into the behavior and habitat of dolphins, fostering an appreciation for the importance of preserving their fragile ecosystem.

## Casela World of Adventures: Where Thrills Meet Nature

For those seeking an adrenaline rush and a connection with nature, Flic-en-Flac offers easy access to Casela World of Adventures, a sprawling adventure park that caters to visitors of all ages. Casela is more than just an amusement park; it's a gateway to exploring the island's rich biodiversity and natural beauty.

One of the highlights of Casela is the exhilarating ziplining experience. As you soar above lush treetops and rugged terrain, you'll gain a bird's-eye view of the island's diverse landscapes. It's an adventure that combines the thrill of flight with the serenity of nature.

If ziplining isn't your cup of tea, Casela has plenty more to offer. Quad biking enthusiasts can embark on off-road expeditions through the park's diverse terrains, from dense forests to open savannahs. The park also features encounters with various wildlife species, including lions and cheetahs, allowing you to get up close and personal with some of the planet's most magnificent creatures.

In addition to the adrenaline-pumping activities, Casela is a paradise for nature lovers. The park's extensive gardens showcase an impressive collection of plants and flowers, offering a serene setting for leisurely walks and picnics.

**Tamarin Village: A Taste of Local Life**

To truly immerse yourself in the local culture and lifestyle, a visit to Tamarin Village is a must. This charming coastal village, just a short drive from Flic-en-Flac, is known for its fishing community and vibrant street food scene.

As you wander through the streets of Tamarin, you'll encounter the sights and sounds of daily life in Mauritius. Colorful fishing boats bob in the bay, their crews preparing for the day's catch. The air is filled with the enticing aromas of freshly grilled seafood and aromatic spices.

Tamarin Village is a culinary paradise for seafood aficionados. You can savor the catch of the day at local seafood shacks, where dishes like grilled octopus, garlic prawns, and fish vindaye are prepared to perfection. The flavors are a delightful fusion of Creole, Indian, and Chinese influences, showcasing the island's rich culinary heritage.

For a unique dining experience, consider joining a beachfront barbecue where you can feast on seafood delights while your toes sink into the warm sands. It's a sensory journey that encapsulates the essence of island living.

In addition to its culinary offerings, Tamarin Village is known for its sense of community and hospitality. Locals are often more than willing to share stories, traditions, and insights into Mauritian life. Don't be surprised if you're invited to join in a game of boules or offered a taste of homemade rum infused with local herbs and spices.

**Flic-en-Flac - Where Every Moment is a Treasure**

Flic-en-Flac and the surrounding west coast of Mauritius are a treasure trove of experiences, each more enchanting than the last. Whether you're seeking relaxation on the golden shores of Flic-en-Flac Beach, embarking on a thrilling dolphin-watching adventure, exploring the natural wonders of Casela World of Adventures, or immersing yourself in the rich culture and flavors of Tamarin Village, every moment spent in this region is a cherished memory in the making.

As you soak in the stunning sunsets that paint the sky with hues of orange and pink, you'll come to understand why Flic-en-Flac is a destination that beckons travelers from around the world. It's a place where the pace of life slows down, where nature and adventure coexist, and where the warm smiles of the locals make you feel truly welcome. Flic-en-Flac isn't just a destination; it's an experience that lingers in your heart long after you've left its shores.

# Chapter 4: Where to Stay

Mauritius offers a diverse range of accommodations to suit every traveler's preferences and budget. Whether you're seeking luxury, looking to save, or craving a unique and intimate experience, you'll find the perfect place to stay on this enchanting island.

## Luxury Resorts and Boutique Hotels

Mauritius, a paradise nestled in the heart of the Indian Ocean, is celebrated for its world-class luxury resorts and boutique hotels that grace its pristine coastline. These establishments represent the pinnacle of tropical indulgence, seamlessly blending elegant architecture, lush gardens, and panoramic ocean vistas to create an atmosphere of unparalleled opulence and relaxation. Here, we delve into the rich tapestry of experiences that await you at these upscale accommodations.

Elegant Suites and Villas: Upon stepping into a luxury resort in Mauritius, you'll find yourself in a world of refined elegance. These establishments typically offer a range of opulent suites and villas, each meticulously designed to provide the utmost comfort and luxury. Many of these accommodations come complete with private pools and direct access to the powdery sands of the island's pristine beaches. Whether you choose a suite overlooking the turquoise waters or a secluded villa hidden among lush tropical foliage, you can expect nothing short of lavish comfort.

Fine Dining: Dining at a luxury resort in Mauritius is a culinary journey through the flavors of the world. On-site restaurants at these establishments are renowned for their excellence, boasting a diverse array of international and Mauritian cuisine. Talented chefs curate menus that celebrate the island's rich culinary heritage, blending local ingredients with global influences to create exquisite dishes. Whether you're savoring freshly caught seafood, indulging in traditional Creole specialties, or exploring international gastronomy, every meal is a gastronomic delight.

Spa and Wellness: Your well-being is a top priority at these resorts, which often feature world-class spas and wellness centers. Here, you can pamper yourself with a wide range of rejuvenating treatments, from traditional Mauritian massages to holistic therapies. The serene spa environments are designed to help you unwind and find inner peace, complemented by expert therapists who tailor treatments to your specific needs. These wellness havens provide an oasis of relaxation, allowing you to rejuvenate both body and soul.

Waterfront Activities: The allure of the Indian Ocean beckons right from your doorstep at these luxury resorts. You can enjoy an array of water-based activities without venturing far. Snorkeling reveals the vibrant marine life of coral reefs just offshore, while diving enthusiasts can explore underwater caves and wrecks. Paddleboarding and kayaking provide tranquil ways to navigate the crystal-clear waters, and sailing excursions offer romantic sunsets or thrilling adventures.

Entertainment and Nightlife: Evenings at luxury resorts in Mauritius come alive with entertainment options to suit your desires. Some establishments host live performances, from traditional Mauritian music and dance to international acts. Themed parties add a touch of excitement to your nights, allowing you to immerse yourself in the local culture or transport you to exotic destinations. For those seeking vibrant nightlife, upscale bars and clubs provide an opportunity to dance the night away or savor expertly crafted cocktails under the starlit sky.

In essence, a stay at a luxury resort in Mauritius is not just a vacation; it's an immersive journey into an oasis of opulence and natural beauty. Here, you can create cherished memories, indulge your senses, and experience the true essence of paradise.

As of my last knowledge update in September 2021, Seychelles is home to a plethora of luxurious resorts and boutique hotels. While I can't provide real-time information, I can offer you a list of some well-known luxury accommodations along with their addresses and a brief description of each. Be sure to verify the latest details, including availability and rates, before planning your stay in Seychelles.

**North Island, a Luxury Collection Resort, Seychelles**
Address: North Island, Seychelles
Description: North Island is an exclusive and environmentally conscious private island resort. With just 11 villas, it offers an ultra-luxurious, all-inclusive experience.

Guests can enjoy pristine beaches, lush forests, and abundant marine life. Each villa is a secluded sanctuary with its own pool and direct beach access.

### Fregate Island Private
Address: Fregate Island Private, Seychelles
Description: Fregate Island is a renowned private island escape. It boasts 16 villas and one presidential villa, all with private pools and dedicated butlers. The island is a sanctuary for nature lovers, home to rare species and lush vegetation. It's also known for its conservation efforts and sustainability initiatives.

### Four Seasons Resort Seychelles at Desroches Island
Address: Desroches Island, Seychelles
Description: Situated on Desroches Island, this Four Seasons property offers an exclusive tropical paradise. The resort features luxurious beachfront suites, villas, and residences. Guests can enjoy water sports, spa treatments, and a variety of dining options in a secluded and idyllic setting.

### Six Senses Zil Pasyon
Address: Félicité Island, Seychelles
Description: Located on Félicité Island, Six Senses Zil Pasyon is an eco-friendly resort offering stunning ocean views and spacious villas with private pools. The resort emphasizes wellness and sustainability, offering spa treatments, yoga sessions, and exquisite dining experiences.

### Constance Lémuria Seychelles
Address: Anse Kerlan, Praslin Island, Seychelles

Description: Constance Lémuria is a luxurious resort on Praslin Island. It features spacious suites and villas, an 18-hole championship golf course, and a stunning beach. Guests can explore the Vallée de Mai Nature Reserve, a UNESCO World Heritage site nearby.

**Raffles Seychelles**
Address: Anse Takamaka, Praslin Island, Seychelles
Description: Raffles Seychelles is nestled on Praslin's southwest coast, offering elegant villas with private plunge pools. The resort boasts a rejuvenating spa, exceptional dining options, and access to pristine beaches and coral reefs.

**Banyan Tree Seychelles**
Address: Anse Intendance, Mahé Island, Seychelles
Description: Located on Mahé Island, Banyan Tree Seychelles offers luxury pool villas with spectacular views of the Indian Ocean. Guests can indulge in spa treatments, fine dining, and water sports while surrounded by lush tropical vegetation.

These are just a few of the luxurious accommodations available in Seychelles. It's advisable to check the most recent information and reviews when planning your stay. Additionally, Seychelles has many more boutique hotels and resorts, each offering a unique and enchanting experience.

## Budget-Friendly Accommodations

Traveling on a budget doesn't mean compromising on comfort or experience in Mauritius. This section is dedicated to helping you find affordable yet enjoyable places to stay on the island.

Guesthouses and Hostels: Mauritius boasts a vibrant guesthouse culture that is ideal for budget-conscious travelers. These guesthouses, often family-run, provide an authentic taste of Mauritian hospitality and culture. Unlike larger hotels, guesthouses offer a more intimate and personalized experience. You'll find yourself welcomed into a warm and inviting atmosphere, where hosts are eager to share their knowledge of the island. Expect cozy rooms with basic amenities, and some guesthouses even offer homemade Mauritian meals, allowing you to savor the local cuisine without splurging on restaurant bills.

Budget Hotels: In popular tourist areas like Grand Baie and Flic en Flac, you can find a variety of budget-friendly hotels and hostels. While these accommodations may not have the opulence of luxury resorts, they provide clean and comfortable rooms for travelers on a tighter budget. Some budget hotels even have swimming pools and on-site restaurants, ensuring a pleasant stay without the high price tag.

Self-Catering Options: If you prefer to have more control over your meals and expenses, consider staying in a self-catering apartment or studio. These options are perfect for travelers who want to cook their meals and have a home away from home. You'll typically find fully equipped kitchens where you can prepare your favorite dishes using fresh ingredients from local markets. This not only saves money but also allows you to experiment with Mauritian flavors.

Backpacker Hostels: For backpackers, Mauritius offers affordable dormitory-style accommodations. These hostels cater to the budget traveler looking for a social atmosphere and a chance to meet fellow adventurers. While the facilities may be more basic, they often come with communal spaces where you can swap stories, plan excursions, and make new friends. Additionally, some backpacker hostels organize group activities and outings, making it easy to explore the island on a budget.

Seychelles is known for its luxurious resorts, but there are also some budget-friendly accommodations that offer comfortable stays without breaking the bank. Here are a few popular options with their addresses and detailed descriptions:

## Green Palm Self Catering Apartments

Address: Anse Aux Pins, Mahe Island, Seychelles
Description: Green Palm Self Catering Apartments offers spacious and well-equipped apartments, perfect for travelers looking for self-catering options. The apartments are nestled in a tropical garden, providing a peaceful atmosphere. Each unit includes a kitchenette, dining area, and a private terrace. Anse Aux Pins Beach is within walking distance, and the property is conveniently located near shops and restaurants.

## Coco Blanche

Address: Anse Royale, Mahe Island, Seychelles

Description: Coco Blanche is a family-run guesthouse located in the charming village of Anse Royale. The guesthouse offers comfortable and affordable rooms, some with ocean views. Guests can enjoy the garden and terrace area, and the property is just a short walk from Anse Royale Beach. The owners provide a warm and welcoming atmosphere, making it an excellent choice for budget-conscious travelers.

## Calypha Guesthouse

Address: Beau Vallon, Mahe Island, Seychelles
Description: Calypha Guesthouse is situated in the popular Beau Vallon area on Mahe Island. It offers clean and cozy rooms with modern amenities. The guesthouse is a short walk from the stunning Beau Vallon Beach, known for its clear waters and water sports activities. Guests can also find various restaurants and shops nearby, making it a convenient choice for travelers.

## Chez Lorna

Address: La Digue, Seychelles
Description: Chez Lorna is a charming guesthouse located on the picturesque La Digue Island. The guesthouse offers affordable and comfortable rooms in a tropical garden setting. It's close to Anse Source d'Argent, one of the most famous beaches in the Seychelles. Guests can explore the island by renting bicycles, which are readily available, and enjoy the laid-back atmosphere of La Digue.

## Palm Beach Hotel

Address: Praslin, Seychelles
Description: Palm Beach Hotel on Praslin Island provides budget-friendly accommodation with a relaxed island vibe. The hotel offers comfortable rooms with essential amenities. It's located near the stunning Anse Volbert Beach, allowing guests easy access to the turquoise waters and beautiful scenery. The hotel's on-site restaurant serves Creole and international cuisine.

These budget-friendly accommodations in Seychelles provide an opportunity to experience the natural beauty of the islands without overspending on lodging. While they may not offer the extravagance of high-end resorts, they make up for it with their warm hospitality and convenient locations near Seychelles' famous beaches and attractions.

In summary, Mauritius provides a range of budget-friendly accommodations that allow you to experience the island without breaking the bank. Whether you choose a guesthouse for an immersive cultural experience, a budget hotel for convenience, a self-catering option for flexibility, or a backpacker hostel for a social atmosphere, you can rest assured that comfort and affordability can coexist in this tropical paradise.

## Unique Stays: Villas and Guesthouses

For those seeking a more personalized and unique experience, Mauritius offers a range of alternative accommodations:

For those travelers who desire a more personalized and unique experience in Mauritius, the island offers a variety of alternative accommodations that go beyond the traditional hotel experience. These options allow you to immerse yourself in the culture, nature, or history of Mauritius in a way that is both memorable and authentic:

Villas by the Sea: Renting a private villa is an excellent choice for those seeking exclusivity and privacy. These villas are often located right along the coast, offering stunning panoramic views of the Indian Ocean. You can expect spacious living areas, well-equipped kitchens, and the luxury of your own pool. It's an ideal option for families, groups of friends, or couples looking for a romantic getaway. Imagine waking up to the sound of waves crashing on the shore, with the turquoise waters just steps away from your doorstep.

Charming Guesthouses: If you're eager to dive into the heart of Mauritian culture, consider staying in a charming guesthouse. These locally-run establishments are typically found in authentic Mauritian communities, away from the bustling tourist areas. Here, you'll have the opportunity to connect with the locals, share stories, and savor homemade Mauritian cuisine. The warm hospitality and personalized service offered by guesthouse hosts create a unique and enriching experience that can't be replicated in larger resorts.

Eco-Lodges and Treehouses: For the eco-conscious traveler, Mauritius boasts a selection of eco-lodges and treehouses nestled in the island's lush, natural landscapes. These accommodations are designed with sustainability in mind, often utilizing renewable energy sources and environmentally friendly practices. Staying in an eco-lodge or treehouse allows you to truly connect with nature. You can wake up to the songs of tropical birds, explore pristine forests, and gaze at the starry skies from your canopy-level abode. It's an opportunity to minimize your environmental footprint while enjoying a peaceful and immersive experience in the wild.

Historical Stays: To step back in time and experience the rich history of Mauritius, consider staying in a beautifully restored colonial-era house. These historical stays offer a glimpse into the island's past, with elegant architecture, antique furnishings, and a sense of nostalgia. You can find these accommodations in various parts of the island, each with its unique historical significance. It's a chance to relive the island's colonial heritage while enjoying modern comforts.

These alternative accommodations in Mauritius cater to travelers with diverse interests and preferences, providing a deeper connection to the island's culture, nature, and history. Whether you choose a private villa by the sea, a charming guesthouse in a local community, an eco-lodge in the wilderness, or a historical stay in a colonial-era house, you'll have the opportunity to create lasting memories and experiences that are truly one-of-a-kind.

# Chapter 5: Savoring Mauritian Cuisine

Mauritian cuisine is a tantalizing blend of flavors and influences from around the world. In this chapter, we'll take a deep dive into the island's culinary scene, exploring the diverse range of dishes that make Mauritius a paradise for food lovers.

## A Culinary Fusion: Influences and Flavors

Mauritian cuisine is a true reflection of the island's rich history and multicultural society. Influences from Africa, India, China, and Europe have all left their mark on the island's food culture. The result is a delightful fusion of flavors and cooking techniques that create unique and unforgettable dishes.

**The Creole Influence: Discover the vibrant and spicy Creole cuisine**

Mauritian Creole cuisine is a vibrant and spicy expression of the island's cultural tapestry. Rooted in African, French, and Indian culinary traditions, Creole dishes are known for their bold flavors and aromatic spices. Here's a closer look at this influential aspect of Mauritian gastronomy:

- Rougaille: One of the most emblematic Creole dishes, Rougaille, is a tomato-based sauce infused with chili peppers, garlic, and ginger. It's commonly used as a base for various recipes, including fish, chicken, or sausages.

- Bouillon: A hearty and flavorful soup, Bouillon combines a variety of ingredients, including meat, vegetables, and spices. It's simmered to perfection, creating a savory and spicy broth that's both comforting and satisfying.

**Indian Inspirations: Explore the aromatic world of Mauritian curries, biryanis, and dholl puri**

The Indian influence on Mauritian cuisine is unmistakable, particularly in the prevalence of fragrant spices and curry-based dishes. The Indian community in Mauritius has enriched the island's culinary landscape with a tantalizing array of flavors:

- Curries: Mauritian curries are a harmonious blend of Indian and Creole cooking styles. You can savor chicken, fish, or vegetable curries, each bursting with a symphony of spices like cumin, coriander, and turmeric.

- Biryanis: These aromatic rice dishes are a testament to Indian culinary mastery. Mauritian biryanis often include tender pieces of meat or seafood marinated in spices and served alongside fragrant, saffron-infused rice.

- Dholl Puri: The quintessential Mauritian street food, Dholl Puri, consists of thin, soft flatbreads stuffed with spicy yellow split pea filling and chutney. It's a flavorful and portable delight.

## Chinese Delicacies: Taste the influence of the Chinese community

The Chinese community in Mauritius has made significant contributions to the island's culinary scene. Their influence is evident in savory dishes that have become beloved staples of Mauritian cuisine:

- Mine Frit: A delightful plate of fried noodles, Mine Frit showcases the Chinese mastery of wok cooking. It's often prepared with a variety of ingredients, including vegetables, meat, and seafood, stir-fried to perfection.

- Bol Renversé: This unique dish features an upside-down bowl of rice with meat or seafood on top, often crowned with a rich sauce. It's a testament to the Chinese art of presentation and flavor harmony.

## European Elegance: Indulge in gourmet European cuisine

Mauritius' European influence is not limited to its beautiful architecture but extends to its fine-dining experiences. European-style cuisine can be savored in upscale restaurants, offering a taste of luxury:

- Coq au Vin: A classic French dish, Coq au Vin features chicken braised in red wine with mushrooms and onions, resulting in a rich and indulgent flavor.

- Bouillabaisse: This Provençal fish stew, hailing from France, is a seafood lover's dream. It combines various types of fish, shellfish, and aromatic herbs in a savory broth.

These European-inspired dishes offer a touch of elegance to Mauritius' culinary landscape, providing a perfect complement to the island's diverse and flavorful offerings. Whether you're indulging in Creole, Indian, Chinese, or European fare, Mauritian cuisine promises a culinary journey like no other.

## Must-Try Dishes and Street Food

### Dholl Puri: A Street Food Sensation

Dholl Puri is the undisputed champion of Mauritian street food. This beloved snack is not just a dish; it's a cultural institution. Imagine a soft, thin flatbread, similar to a crepe, but with a unique Mauritian twist. It's made from ground split peas and flour, resulting in a delicate, slightly crispy outer layer that envelopes a savory, spiced filling.

The Experience: As you stroll through bustling marketplaces or along the sandy shores, you'll encounter street vendors expertly crafting dholl puris on hot griddles. The fragrance of the flatbreads wafts through the air, drawing you closer. You can choose from a variety of fillings, such as curried vegetables, chutney, pickles, and sometimes even a choice of meats. The softness of the flatbread contrasts perfectly with the textures and flavors of the fillings, creating a delightful explosion of taste in your mouth.

## Octopus Curry: A Seafood Lover's Delight

For seafood enthusiasts, Octopus Curry is a must-try Mauritian dish that will leave your taste buds tingling. This spicy seafood curry is a harmonious blend of locally caught octopus and a medley of spices, resulting in a rich and flavorful concoction.

The Experience: Whether you dine at a seaside shack or a high-end restaurant, you'll find variations of this dish on nearly every Mauritian menu. The octopus is tenderized and slow-cooked in a fragrant curry sauce, often served with fluffy white rice or a warm bread called "pain maison." The sauce combines elements of Indian, Creole, and Chinese flavors, creating a uniquely Mauritian taste. The tender octopus absorbs the flavors of the curry, resulting in a sumptuous and unforgettable meal.

## Gateaux Piments: A Fiery Snack Sensation

Gateaux Piments are the perfect snack for those who enjoy a bit of heat in their food. These small, fiery chili cakes are an essential part of Mauritian street food culture.

The Experience: Picture deep-fried balls of ground split peas mixed with green chilies and spices, giving them their distinctive spicy kick. The exterior is crispy, while the inside is wonderfully soft. They are often served in small paper bags, making them an ideal on-the-go snack. Locals and visitors alike relish the contrast between the crispy shell and the fiery, flavorful interior. Some enjoy them with a dollop of chutney for an extra burst of flavor.

## Boulettes: Dumplings with a Mauritian Twist

Boulettes are another delightful treat in Mauritius, offering a wide range of fillings and flavors. These dumplings can be either steamed or fried, providing diverse textural experiences.

The Experience: When you order boulettes in Mauritius, you embark on a culinary adventure. You can choose from various fillings, including pork, shrimp, chicken, or vegetables. These fillings are mixed with aromatic spices and encased in a thin, doughy wrapper. Steamed boulettes are soft and delicate, allowing the flavors of the filling to shine through. On the other hand, fried boulettes offer a contrast of crispy and tender textures. They are often served with a side of dipping sauce, enhancing the overall experience.

## Bouillon Blanc: A Hearty Comfort Dish

If you're seeking comfort in a bowl, look no further than Bouillon Blanc. This is the quintessential Mauritian comfort food, a warm and nourishing broth that's perfect for soothing the soul.

The Experience: Bouillon Blanc translates to "white broth," and it's exactly what it sounds like. This comforting dish consists of a clear, flavorful broth filled with a medley of vegetables and meat, often including chicken or pork. It's seasoned with a delicate balance of herbs and spices, resulting in a light yet satisfying flavor. Many Mauritians cherish this dish as a home-cooked specialty, and it's often served with rice or bread, making it a complete and hearty meal.

## Roti Chaud: Warm and Fluffy Flatbreads

Roti Chaud, which translates to "hot bread" in English, is a popular street food in Mauritius. These warm, fluffy flatbreads are similar to Indian rotis and are often served with various fillings.

The Experience: Imagine a freshly baked flatbread filled with delightful combinations like curried vegetables, chutney, and sometimes meats like chicken or lamb. It's like a portable, flavorful meal that you can enjoy on the go. The contrast between the soft, warm bread and the savory fillings is simply irresistible.

## Farata: Thin and Foldable Crepes

Farata is another street food sensation in Mauritius. These thin, foldable crepes are made from a simple batter of flour, water, and a pinch of salt, and they're a versatile canvas for various fillings.

The Experience: You'll often find vendors expertly flipping and folding these crepes as they prepare orders. Fillings can range from spicy curries to simple sugar and butter, offering both savory and sweet options. Farata is a beloved snack or light meal that's a hit with locals and tourists alike.

## Mine Frit: Mauritian-Style Chow Mein

Mine Frit is a delightful Mauritian take on chow mein. It's a stir-fried noodle dish that's been infused with the island's unique flavors.

The Experience: Served piping hot, Mine Frit typically features egg noodles stir-fried with a medley of vegetables, spices, and your choice of protein, such as chicken, shrimp, or tofu. The dish is often flavored with soy sauce and a hint of chili for that signature Mauritian kick. It's a comforting and satisfying option for noodle lovers.

## Vindaye: A Tangy Pickled Delight

Vindaye is a traditional Mauritian dish known for its tangy and spicy flavors. It's a pickling method that's applied to various proteins, most commonly fish or octopus.

The Experience: To make Vindaye, the main ingredient is marinated in a blend of vinegar, mustard seeds, turmeric, and spices. The result is a piquant, flavorful dish that's both tangy and spicy. It's often served with rice or bread, making it a distinctive and delicious Mauritian specialty.

## 5. Tamarind Juice: A Refreshing Beverage

While not a dish, Tamarind Juice is a quintessential Mauritian beverage that's both refreshing and unique. Tamarind is a tropical fruit with a tangy-sweet flavor.

The Experience: Tamarind Juice is made by blending tamarind pulp with water and sugar. The result is a thirst-quenching drink with a sweet and sour taste that's perfect for cooling down on a hot day. It's often served chilled and pairs wonderfully with spicy Mauritian dishes.

## Coconut Chutney: A Flavorful Condiment

Coconut chutney is a common condiment in Mauritian cuisine. It's a versatile accompaniment that adds a burst of flavor to various dishes.

The Experience: This chutney is made from grated coconut mixed with spices, chili peppers, and sometimes a touch of lime juice. It can vary in spiciness, depending on your preference. It's often served alongside dholl puri, farata, and other dishes, adding a delightful tropical twist to your meal.

Each of these dishes tells a story of Mauritius' diverse cultural influences and its passionate love affair with food. When you embark on a culinary journey through Mauritius, you're not just indulging your taste buds; you're immersing yourself in the heart and soul of the island. So, take your time, savor every bite, and let the flavors of Mauritius enchant you.

# Dining Etiquette and Tips

Mauritian dining etiquette is a blend of various traditions, but it's generally relaxed and informal. Here are some tips to enhance your dining experience:

**Respect Local Customs: Remember to dress modestly when visiting more traditional areas or religious sites.**

In Mauritius, modesty is highly valued, especially when you're exploring traditional villages or visiting religious sites like temples and mosques. Here's what you should keep in mind:

- Clothing: When entering these areas, it's essential to cover your shoulders and knees. Both men and women should avoid wearing clothing that is too revealing or too short. Loose-fitting, comfortable attire is a good choice.

- Remove Shoes: It's customary to remove your shoes before entering certain religious places, so be prepared to do so. You'll often find designated areas for this purpose.

- Head Coverings: In some temples, covering your head might be a sign of respect. It's a good idea to carry a scarf or a hat just in case it's required.

**Tipping: Tipping is appreciated but not mandatory. A 10% service charge is often included in the bill at restaurants, but extra tips are welcomed for exceptional service.**

Tipping in Mauritius is a way to show appreciation for good service, and it's generally well-received. However, it's not obligatory. Here are some details on tipping:

- Service Charge: Many restaurants include a 10% service charge in the bill. This charge is intended to go to the staff. It's your choice whether to leave additional tips.

- Exceptional Service: If you receive exceptional service and want to show your appreciation, leaving an additional tip is a nice gesture. It could be around 5-10% of the total bill.

- Tipping Etiquette: It's common to hand the tip directly to the server or leave it on the table if there's no service charge. In hotels, you might leave tips for the cleaning staff as well.

**Try Everything: Don't be shy to try a bit of everything. Mauritian cuisine offers a variety of flavors, so be adventurous!**

Mauritian cuisine is a delightful journey of tastes and textures. Here's why you should embrace culinary adventure:

- Diverse Flavors: Mauritian cuisine is a reflection of the island's multicultural history, offering a wide range of flavors and ingredients. From spicy Creole dishes to savory Indian curries, there's something for every palate.

- Local Specialties: Each region has its own unique specialties, so trying local dishes is a great way to explore the island's culture.

- Street Food: Some of the most delicious and authentic Mauritian food can be found at street food stalls. Don't miss the chance to savor dholl puri, samosas, and gateaux piments.

**Street Food Caution: While street food is delicious, make sure the vendor's hygiene standards are up to par before indulging.**

Street food in Mauritius is a treat for your taste buds, but it's crucial to ensure your food is prepared safely. Here's how:

- Cleanliness: Look for vendors who maintain clean and hygienic cooking spaces. If the stall appears dirty or unkempt, it's best to find another one.

- Fresh Ingredients: Opt for stalls that use fresh ingredients and cook food to order. Avoid pre-cooked items that have been sitting out for a long time.

- Local Recommendations: Ask locals or fellow travelers for recommendations on trusted street food vendors. They can point you to the best spots.

**Local Beverages: Complement your meals with local drinks like Alouda (a sweet milk-based beverage) or Phoenix Beer.**

To complete your Mauritian dining experience, don't forget to explore the island's local beverages:

- Alouda: This sweet and creamy milk-based drink is flavored with ingredients like basil seeds, agar-agar jelly, and vanilla. It's incredibly refreshing on a hot day.

- Phoenix Beer: Mauritius has its own beer brand, Phoenix Beer. It's a popular choice to accompany your meals, especially seafood dishes.

- Rum: If you're a fan of spirits, try some of the local rum varieties. Mauritius produces some excellent rum, which you can enjoy straight or in cocktails.

Remember, the local beverages add a unique dimension to your culinary journey, allowing you to savor the full spectrum of Mauritian flavors.

Savoring Mauritian cuisine is not just about enjoying food; it's a cultural experience that connects you with the island's history and people. So, prepare your taste buds for a culinary journey you won't soon forget.

# Chapter 6: Immerse in Culture and History

Mauritius is not only a haven for sun-seekers but also a treasure trove of culture and history waiting to be explored. In this chapter, we delve into the island's rich heritage, vibrant traditions, and its captivating past.

## Heritage Sites and Museums

Mauritius boasts a fascinating blend of cultural influences, evident in its numerous heritage sites and museums. Explore these historical gems to get a deeper understanding of the island's multifaceted history:

## Aapravasi Ghat: A Testament to Resilience and History

The Aapravasi Ghat, a UNESCO World Heritage Site, stands as an enduring testament to a pivotal chapter in Mauritius' history. Located in Port Louis, this site is more than just a collection of historic buildings; it is a poignant reminder of the island's colonial past and the indomitable spirit of its people.

### Historical Significance

During the 19th century, Mauritius, like many other colonies, was in dire need of labor to support its burgeoning sugar industry. The British colonial authorities turned to indentured labor, a system that brought thousands of laborers to the island from various parts of the world, including India, China, Africa, and Southeast Asia.

The Aapravasi Ghat served as the primary immigration depot for these indentured laborers. It was here that they disembarked from their arduous journeys, enduring weeks or even months at sea, in search of better prospects. The name "Aapravasi" itself translates to "immigrant" in Hindi, a language spoken by many of these laborers.

**Architectural Heritage**

The site features a collection of well-preserved buildings that once played crucial roles in the immigration process. The main building, with its striking red brick façade, served as the central administrative office. It was here that laborers were registered, medically examined, and assigned to their respective plantations.

Visitors can explore the barracks where laborers were temporarily housed, gaining insights into the harsh living conditions they faced. A small shrine, known as the "Coolie Ghat Temple," pays homage to the laborers' diverse religious backgrounds, emphasizing the site's multicultural history.

**Resilience and Cultural Contribution**

The Aapravasi Ghat tells a story of incredible resilience. Despite the adversity they faced, these indentured laborers and their descendants made significant contributions to the island's cultural and economic landscape. They brought with them a rich tapestry of traditions, languages, and cuisines that continue to shape Mauritius today.

As you walk through the Aapravasi Ghat, you can almost feel the echoes of the past. It's a place where history comes alive, where you can reflect on the hardships endured by those who came seeking a better life and the enduring spirit that carried them through.

## Eureka House: A Glimpse into Colonial Opulence

Just a short drive from the bustling streets of Port Louis, Eureka House offers a captivating journey back in time. This beautifully preserved Creole mansion provides an intimate glimpse into the opulent lifestyle of the 19th-century colonial elite in Mauritius.

**A Colonial Jewel**

Eureka House, also known as Maison Eureka, is a colonial mansion set amidst lush gardens and surrounded by the Moka Mountains. It was built in the 1830s by a wealthy Frenchman named Joseph Daurel. The mansion's architecture is a stunning blend of European and Creole influences, showcasing intricate wooden fretwork, wide verandas, and a distinctive red-tiled roof.

## Opulence and History

Stepping inside Eureka House is like entering a time capsule of colonial extravagance. The interior is adorned with antique furniture, exquisite china, and period decor. The mansion boasts 109 doors and windows, each designed to capture a different view of the surrounding landscape.

The mansion's opulent past is palpable in every room. Visitors can explore the various living spaces, including the dining room, music room, and library, all furnished with pieces that transport you to the 19th century. The gardens surrounding the mansion are equally enchanting, with a collection of rare plant species and a natural spring waterfall.

## Cultural Connections

Eureka House is not only a testament to colonial wealth but also a place where different cultures converged. The mansion's history is tied to the island's diverse population, and it's a place where you can learn about the interactions between European colonizers, African slaves, and Indian and Chinese laborers.

# Château de Labourdonnais: Unraveling the Sugar Plantation Era

Château de Labourdonnais stands as a grand monument to Mauritius' sugar plantation era, a period that played a pivotal role in shaping the island's history and economy.

## Historical Roots

Located in Mapou, in the northern part of Mauritius, Château de Labourdonnais was constructed in the 1850s by Christian Wiehe. Wiehe, a wealthy landowner, was part of the island's sugar aristocracy, and the château was designed to showcase his affluence.

## A Window into the Past

Today, Château de Labourdonnais offers visitors a unique opportunity to step back in time and explore the opulent world of a 19th-century sugar baron. The château is a stunning example of French colonial architecture, with its elegant verandas, ornate ironwork, and meticulously landscaped gardens.

Inside, the château has been lovingly restored to its former glory, with period-appropriate furnishings and decor. As you wander through the rooms, you'll gain insights into the lifestyle of the plantation owners and the laborers who toiled in the sugarcane fields.

## Sugar Production History

A visit to Château de Labourdonnais wouldn't be complete without delving into the history of sugar production in Mauritius. The estate includes a working sugar factory, where you can see the traditional methods used to extract sugarcane juice and process it into sugar. The guides provide fascinating insights into the island's sugar industry and its evolution over the centuries.

# Blue Penny Museum: A Philatelic and Cultural Treasure

The Blue Penny Museum, nestled in the heart of Port Louis, is a hidden gem that not only houses one of the world's rarest stamps but also offers a captivating journey through Mauritius' philatelic history and its rich cultural heritage.

## The Star of the Show

The crown jewel of the Blue Penny Museum is undoubtedly the "Blue Penny," a postage stamp that has achieved legendary status among collectors worldwide. Printed in 1847, the Blue Penny is considered one of the rarest and most valuable stamps in existence. Its vivid blue color and distinctive design make it a symbol of Mauritius' philatelic heritage.

## Exploring Mauritius Through Stamps

While the Blue Penny may be the museum's most famous exhibit, it's just the beginning of the stamp-related treasures on display. The museum features an extensive collection of postage stamps that trace the history and evolution of Mauritius through the years.

## Art and Culture

Beyond its philatelic treasures, the Blue Penny Museum is a celebration of Mauritian art and culture. The museum's exhibits showcase the island's vibrant artistic traditions, including sculptures, paintings, and contemporary artworks.

**A Cultural Experience**

Visitors to the Blue Penny Museum can immerse themselves in the stories and legends that have shaped Mauritian culture. The museum often hosts temporary exhibitions that highlight various aspects of the island's heritage, from its multiculturalism to its natural wonders.

These four cultural and historical landmarks - Aapravasi Ghat, Eureka House, Château de Labourdonnais, and the Blue Penny Museum - offer visitors a unique opportunity to delve into the multifaceted history, culture, and heritage of Mauritius. Each of these sites tells a different story, from the struggles of indentured laborers to the opulence of colonial elites and the artistry of philatelic history. Together, they provide a comprehensive and enriching experience that deepens one's appreciation for this enchanting island nation.

# Traditional Music, Dance, and Festivals

Mauritian culture is a dynamic fusion of influences from India, Africa, Europe, and Asia, and it comes alive through its vibrant music, dance, and festivals:

# Sega Dance: The Rhythmic Heartbeat of Mauritius

When you set foot on the picturesque island of Mauritius, you're not just greeted by the sun-kissed beaches and azure waters; you're welcomed into a world where culture and music dance together in the gentle sea breeze. One of the most captivating aspects of Mauritian culture is the Sega dance, a traditional music and dance form that embodies the spirit of the island.

## A Melodic Introduction to Sega

Sega is the soulful heartbeat of Mauritius. It's a genre of music and a dance style that has been passed down through generations, deeply ingrained in the island's history and heritage. Rooted in the cultural fusion of African rhythms, Creole language, and French and Indian influences, Sega is a reflection of Mauritius' rich diversity.

## The Rhythmic Beats

The Sega dance is all about sensuous rhythms and graceful movements. It's often performed at beachside bonfires under the starlit sky, setting a perfect ambiance for the experience. The beat of the music is typically set by traditional instruments like the ravanne (a tambourine-like drum), the triangle, and the maravanne (a rattle). Musicians and singers come together to create a hypnotic melody that resonates with the heart and soul of the island.

As the music starts, dancers join in, their hips swaying gracefully to the rhythm. The dance is a mesmerizing display of fluidity, with women often dressed in colorful skirts that twirl gracefully as they move. The men, too, display their prowess in the dance, their feet tapping to the beat as they keep up with the intricate steps.

### A Cultural Experience

Sega is not just a performance; it's a cultural experience. It's a reflection of the island's history, where African slaves, Indian indentured laborers, and European settlers came together to create a unique identity. The lyrics of Sega songs often tell stories of love, sorrow, and everyday life on the island, making it a powerful medium for storytelling and cultural preservation.

If you have the opportunity to witness a Sega dance performance during your visit to Mauritius, you'll find yourself drawn into the hypnotic rhythms and the heartfelt expressions of the dancers. It's an experience that transcends entertainment; it's a window into the soul of the island.

## Chinese Lion Dance: A Spectacle of Tradition and Luck

In the colorful tapestry of Mauritius' cultural celebrations, the Chinese Lion Dance stands out as a symbol of good luck and prosperity. While the island is primarily known for its African, Indian, and Creole heritage, its Chinese community adds a unique layer of cultural diversity, especially during Chinese New Year and other festive occasions.

## *The Dance of the Lions*

The Chinese Lion Dance is a visually stunning and acrobatic performance that is deeply rooted in Chinese folklore and tradition. It's a dance of two performers, one at the head and the other at the tail of the lion costume. This costume, often adorned with vibrant colors and intricate patterns, is designed to resemble a lion and is believed to bring good fortune and ward off evil spirits.

The performance is a choreographed blend of martial arts, dance, and music. The lion moves with graceful agility, mimicking various gestures and expressions that symbolize aspects of Chinese mythology. It's a mesmerizing display of skill and coordination as the lion leaps, rolls, and interacts with the audience.

## *Chinese New Year and Beyond*

While Chinese New Year is the most prominent occasion for the Lion Dance in Mauritius, you can also witness this vibrant performance during other Chinese festivals and celebrations. The dance is often accompanied by the rhythmic sounds of drums, cymbals, and gongs, creating an atmosphere of festivity and jubilation.

Beyond its entertainment value, the Chinese Lion Dance is deeply symbolic. It's believed to bring good luck, prosperity, and happiness to those who witness it. It's not uncommon for businesses and individuals to invite lion dance troupes to their premises to perform during special occasions or to mark the opening of a new venture.

# Maha Shivaratri: A Profound Hindu Festival

Mauritius is a melting pot of cultures and religions, and one of the most significant Hindu festivals celebrated on the island is Maha Shivaratri. This festival, dedicated to Lord Shiva, is a testament to the deep spiritual roots that thrive in the hearts of the Mauritian people.

### A Night of Devotion

Maha Shivaratri, which translates to "The Great Night of Lord Shiva," is celebrated with great fervor and devotion by the local Hindu community. The festival typically falls in the months of February or March, depending on the lunar calendar. What makes this festival truly remarkable is the tradition of night-long prayers and pilgrimages to the sacred crater lake of Grand Bassin.

Devotees, many of whom have observed a period of fasting and abstinence leading up to the festival, embark on a spiritual journey to Grand Bassin. Some pilgrims walk barefoot for miles as an act of penance and devotion. As they approach the lake, their faces often painted with sacred ash, they carry offerings to Lord Shiva. These offerings include items like fruits, flowers, coconuts, and even pots of milk.

### *The Sacred Lake of Grand Bassin*

Grand Bassin, also known as Ganga Talao, is a stunning volcanic crater lake nestled amidst lush green hills. It's considered to be a sacred spot where the waters are believed to be connected to the holy Ganges River in India. For the devotees, taking a dip in the waters of Grand Bassin during Maha Shivaratri is an act of spiritual purification and a way to seek Lord Shiva's blessings.

As night falls, the atmosphere around Grand Bassin becomes electric. Pilgrims and visitors light oil lamps and candles, creating a mesmerizing spectacle of flickering lights. The air is filled with the scent of incense, and the rhythmic chanting of prayers adds to the mystical ambiance.

## Cavadee Festival: A Testimony of Devotion

The Cavadee Festival is a remarkable Tamil Hindu celebration that showcases the depth of faith and devotion within the Mauritian Tamil community. This festival, often marked by acts of body piercing and penance, is a unique cultural event that is both awe-inspiring and deeply spiritual.

### *A Test of Devotion*

The Cavadee Festival is celebrated on the full moon day in the Tamil month of Thai (usually in January or February). Devotees, dressed in saffron-colored attire, undertake a pilgrimage to a temple dedicated to Lord Muruga, also known as Lord Subramanya. These pilgrims carry a kavadi, a semi-circular decorated wooden arch, on their shoulders as an offering to the deity.

What makes the Cavadee Festival truly astonishing is the act of body piercing that many devotees willingly undertake. Some participants have skewers and hooks pierced through their tongues, cheeks, or other parts of their bodies. This act is seen as a way to demonstrate their dedication and to seek blessings from the deity for themselves and their families.

### *The Journey of Sacrifice*

As the devotees begin their journey to the temple, the weight of the kavadi and the pain from their piercings serve as a physical reminder of their devotion. Family members and fellow devotees often accompany them, offering support and encouragement along the way. The procession is accompanied by the rhythmic sounds of drums, music, and chanting, creating an atmosphere of spiritual fervor.

Upon reaching the temple, devotees undergo a purification ceremony before making their offerings to Lord Muruga. They may perform various rituals and prayers, seeking blessings for their well-being and the well-being of their loved ones.

### *A Festival of Unity*

The Cavadee Festival is not just a religious event; it's a celebration of unity within the Tamil Hindu community in Mauritius. Families and friends come together to support those participating in the festival, and the entire community is involved in the preparations and festivities.

Mauritius' cultural diversity shines through in its vibrant celebrations and festivals. From the sensuous rhythms of the Sega dance to the awe-inspiring acts of devotion during Maha Shivaratri and the Cavadee Festival, these cultural expressions are a testament to the island's rich heritage and the harmonious coexistence of different cultures and religions. Experiencing these traditions firsthand during your visit to Mauritius will not only leave you with unforgettable memories but also a deeper appreciation for the island's cultural tapestry.

# Learning About the Island's History

Understanding Mauritius' history is essential to truly appreciate its present-day cultural tapestry. Here's how you can delve into the island's history:

## National History Museum: Unveiling Mauritius' Past

Nestled within the heart of Port Louis, the National History Museum of Mauritius stands as an iconic testament to the island's rich and diverse history. For any traveler with a penchant for delving deep into the past, this museum is an essential stop on your journey through this captivating island nation.

### A Glimpse into the Museum

As you approach the museum, you'll immediately be struck by its stately architecture, which echoes the colonial heritage of the island. The museum, housed in a grand building that exudes an air of historical significance, is a veritable treasure trove of artifacts and exhibits that eloquently narrate Mauritius' remarkable journey from its volcanic origins to the bustling modern society it is today.

### Tracing Mauritius' Volcanic Birth

One of the most intriguing aspects of Mauritius is its geological history, and the museum's exhibits provide an engaging starting point. Through meticulously curated displays, visitors are transported back in time to witness the island's tumultuous birth from the depths of the ocean, as volcanic activity forged the very land beneath their feet. Rare geological specimens and informative panels explain the island's unique formation, highlighting its isolation in the vast Indian Ocean.

### The Tale of Indigenous Inhabitants

Moving forward in time, the museum pays homage to the island's first inhabitants – the indigenous fauna and flora. Visitors can marvel at fossils and remnants of giant tortoises and dodos, species that once thrived on the island but sadly met their extinction due to human arrival and colonization.

## Colonization and Slavery: A Dark Chapter

The exhibits then take a somber turn, shedding light on the dark era of colonization and slavery. Detailed dioramas and artifacts from this period paint a vivid picture of the hardships endured by the enslaved population and the lasting impact of this painful history on Mauritius' culture and society.

## From Sugar Plantations to Independence

The museum meticulously chronicles the island's transition from a sugar-dependent economy under French and later British rule to its eventual path to independence. This transformation is vividly portrayed through artifacts from the sugar plantation era, including equipment used in sugar production and the dwellings of the laborers who toiled in the fields.

## Independence and Modernization

Mauritius' journey to independence in 1968 marked a turning point in its history, and the museum dedicates a section to this pivotal moment. Visitors can explore the political milestones, leaders, and events that led to the birth of a new nation.

## Contemporary Developments and Cultural Diversity

The museum doesn't just linger in the past but also casts an eye on the vibrant present of Mauritius. Exhibits showcase the island's cultural diversity, reflecting the various communities that have contributed to its unique identity. From religious celebrations and festivals to contemporary art and music, you'll gain an appreciation for the vibrant tapestry of Mauritian culture.

## Local Guides and Cultural Tours: A Personal Journey Through History

While the National History Museum offers a comprehensive overview of Mauritius' history, nothing quite compares to the immersive experience of exploring the island's historical landmarks with a knowledgeable local guide. Engaging a local guide can be a transformative experience, as they breathe life into the stories and legends that surround Mauritius' past.

### What to Expect with Local Guides

- In-Depth Insights: Local guides are passionate storytellers who possess a deep understanding of Mauritius' history. They provide nuanced insights that go beyond the museum exhibits, offering a personal and cultural perspective on the island's past.

- Historical Landmarks: Your journey with a local guide may take you to historical sites like the Aapravasi Ghat, where indentured laborers first set foot on the island, or to the ruins of old sugar mills that whisper tales of the sugar plantation era.

- Captivating Stories: These guides have an incredible knack for narrating captivating stories that transport you back in time. From tales of pirate lore to the struggles of enslaved populations and the island's road to independence, each story is a window into Mauritius' past.

- Cultural Immersion: Beyond history, local guides can introduce you to the island's living culture. You might find yourself participating in traditional rituals, tasting authentic Mauritian cuisine, or witnessing local festivals and celebrations.

## Reading and Research: A Deeper Dive

For the intellectually curious traveler, delving into books and research materials about Mauritius' history is an excellent way to gain a comprehensive understanding of the island's past, including its colonial legacy, path to independence, and contemporary developments.

Recommended Books and Resources

- "Mauritius: Its Creole Language - The Ultimate Creole Phrase Book and Dictionary" by Daniel Austin: This book provides a deep dive into the Creole language, which is a reflection of the island's diverse cultural influences.

- "The Making of Modern Mauritius" by Lindsay Rivière: Offering a comprehensive look at the history of Mauritius from colonization to modern times, this book is an essential read for history enthusiasts.

- "Mauritius: Remote Control" by Linda Rast: This insightful book explores Mauritius' political and economic transformation after gaining independence.

- Online Archives and Academic Journals: Academic journals and online archives offer valuable historical research materials, including documents and articles that delve into specific aspects of Mauritius' history.

By engaging with these resources, you can deepen your appreciation of Mauritius' complex history, its vibrant culture, and the unique blend of influences that have shaped this captivating island nation. Whether you explore through museum exhibits, local guides, or extensive research, Mauritius' rich history is a narrative waiting to be discovered and embraced.

# Chapter 7: Breathtaking Natural Wonders

Mauritius, often referred to as paradise on Earth, boasts a stunning array of natural wonders that will leave you spellbound. In this chapter, we will take you on a journey through the island's most enchanting natural attractions, from its pristine beaches to the captivating underwater world and lush interior landscapes.

## Beaches of Paradise: White Sands and Azure Waters

Picture yourself on a postcard-perfect beach: powdery white sands stretching as far as the eye can see, gently kissed by the crystal-clear, turquoise waters of the Indian Ocean. Mauritius is renowned for its exceptional beaches, each with its unique charm. Here, we'll introduce you to some of the most beautiful coastal spots on the island, including:

### Flic en Flac Beach: A Haven for Sun-Seekers and Water Sports Enthusiasts

Flic en Flac Beach, often simply referred to as Flic en Flac, is one of Mauritius' most popular and beloved beach destinations. Situated on the west coast of the island, it is easily accessible from the major towns and cities, making it a convenient choice for both tourists and locals alike.

### *Best Times to Visit Flic en Flac:*

Flic en Flac enjoys a tropical climate, with warm temperatures year-round. However, the best time to visit this paradise on the west coast is during the dry season, which typically runs from May to December. During this period, you can expect less rainfall and more sunny days, ensuring optimal beach conditions.

### *Activities to Enjoy:*

- Sunbathing and Swimming: The beach is renowned for its long stretch of powdery white sand and calm, clear waters. Whether you're looking to soak up the sun, take a leisurely swim, or build sandcastles with the family, Flic en Flac offers a picture-perfect setting.

- Water Sports: For the more adventurous traveler, Flic en Flac provides an array of water sports activities. From snorkeling and scuba diving to windsurfing and kiteboarding, there are opportunities aplenty to dive into the Indian Ocean's warm waters.

- Dolphin Watching: Flic en Flac is a popular departure point for dolphin watching tours. These excursions allow you to witness pods of playful dolphins in their natural habitat, creating unforgettable memories.

- Beachfront Dining: Numerous beachfront restaurants and bars offer delectable Mauritian cuisine, including fresh seafood. Enjoy a romantic dinner or a sunset cocktail with your toes in the sand.

### *Insider Tips for a Perfect Beach Day:*

- Arrive Early: To secure the best spot on the beach, arrive early in the morning before the crowds descend. This will also give you the opportunity to witness a breathtaking sunrise over the ocean.

- Stay Hydrated: Mauritius can get hot, especially during the peak of the day. Make sure to stay hydrated by drinking plenty of water and applying sunscreen regularly.

- Explore Tamarin Bay: If you're a surfer, don't miss the chance to catch some waves at nearby Tamarin Bay, a renowned surf spot located just a short drive from Flic en Flac.

## Belle Mare Plage: Known for its Long Stretches of Soft Sand and Vibrant Marine Life

On the opposite side of the island, nestled on the east coast, lies the idyllic Belle Mare Plage. This beach is famous for its long expanses of soft, powdery sand that seem to stretch endlessly, and its waters are teeming with marine life, making it a paradise for beachgoers and water enthusiasts alike.

### Best Times to Visit Belle Mare Plage:
Similar to Flic en Flac, Belle Mare Plage is most enjoyable during the dry season from May to December. During this

period, the east coast benefits from pleasant weather conditions, making it an ideal time for beach activities.

**Activities to Enjoy:**

- Beachcombing: Belle Mare Plage's extensive shoreline is perfect for long walks along the beach. Collect seashells or simply relish in the feeling of soft sand beneath your feet.

- Swimming and Snorkeling: The calm and crystal-clear waters of Belle Mare Plage are ideal for swimming, and the coral reefs just offshore create an underwater wonderland for snorkelers. Colorful fish and other marine creatures await your exploration.

- Catamaran Cruises: Set sail on a catamaran cruise from Belle Mare Plage to explore nearby islands and islets. These trips often include opportunities for snorkeling, barbecue lunches, and relaxation in secluded lagoons.

- Luxury Resorts: Belle Mare Plage is home to some of Mauritius' most luxurious beachfront resorts, offering world-class amenities and spa services. Consider a day pass to experience their pampering facilities.

**Insider Tips for a Perfect Beach Day:**

- Early Morning Stroll: Take a tranquil early morning stroll along the beach to witness a breathtaking

sunrise. The soft hues of dawn reflecting on the calm sea are a sight to behold.
- Pack a Picnic: While there are restaurants nearby, consider packing a picnic to fully enjoy the beauty of Belle Mare Plage. Don't forget to bring your reusable water bottles and sunscreen.

- Water Shoes: If you plan to explore the coral reefs, bring water shoes to protect your feet from sharp coral and rocks.

## Le Morne Beach: Home to One of the Island's Most Iconic Landmarks, Le Morne Brabant

Le Morne Beach, located on the southwestern tip of Mauritius, is not only a picturesque stretch of coastline but also the backdrop for one of the island's most iconic landmarks, Le Morne Brabant. This UNESCO World Heritage site carries immense historical and cultural significance, making it a must-visit during your time on the island.

### Best Times to Visit Le Morne Beach:
The weather on the southwest coast tends to be sunny and dry throughout the year. However, the months from April to November are often recommended for a visit, as they provide more stable conditions for outdoor activities.

### Activities to Enjoy:

- Hiking Le Morne Brabant: The towering basaltic monolith of Le Morne Brabant invites adventurous hikers. Trekking to the summit rewards you with panoramic views of the surrounding lagoon and coastline.

- Kite Surfing: Le Morne is renowned as one of the world's best kite surfing spots. The consistent trade winds and shallow lagoon create ideal conditions for both beginners and experts.

- Beachfront Yoga: Many resorts in the area offer yoga and wellness retreats right on the beach. Find your inner peace while surrounded by the natural beauty of Le Morne.

- Historical Exploration: Delve into the history of Le Morne Brabant, which was once a refuge for escaped slaves. Learn about its cultural significance and the stories of the maroons who sought sanctuary here.

## *Insider Tips for a Perfect Beach Day:*

- Respect the Natural Environment: As a UNESCO site, Le Morne is protected, and it's essential to respect the natural surroundings. Stay on designated paths during hikes, and avoid leaving any trace of your visit.

- Sunset Views: If you can time your visit for sunset, the view from Le Morne Brabant is truly breathtaking. However, ensure you descend the mountain well before dark, as the trails can be challenging after sunset.

- Local Eateries: Explore nearby villages for authentic Mauritian cuisine. Try local specialties like dholl puri and samosas from food vendors for a taste of the island's flavors.

Le Morne Beach and its iconic backdrop offer a unique blend of adventure, history, and natural beauty. It's a place where you can immerse yourself in the culture and outdoor activities that make Mauritius such a captivating destination.

# Exploring Coral Reefs and Marine Life

Mauritius has a secret world hidden beneath its azure waters that is nothing short of enchanting. Beyond its picturesque beaches and lush landscapes, the island's coral reefs and marine life beckon those who seek to explore the aquatic wonders. In this section, we'll immerse ourselves in the mesmerizing world beneath the surface:

**Snorkeling and Diving Hotspots: Explore the Coral Gardens and Encounter Colorful Fish**

Mauritius is blessed with an extensive coral reef system that encircles the island, creating a haven for marine biodiversity. For both novice snorkelers and seasoned divers, there are abundant opportunities to delve into this vibrant underwater realm.

Coral Gardens: Picture yourself floating effortlessly above a kaleidoscope of colors as you snorkel or dive amidst the coral gardens. These delicate ecosystems teem with life, from intricate coral formations to a dazzling array of tropical fish. We'll guide you to some of the best spots to witness this underwater splendor, providing insights into the unique marine life you may encounter.

## Turtle Watching: Learn About the Conservation Efforts to Protect These Majestic Creatures

One of the most heartwarming and educational experiences in Mauritius is encountering the island's resident sea turtles. These magnificent creatures, including the Hawksbill and Green turtles, grace the shores of Mauritius, especially during nesting seasons.

Conservation Efforts: Discover the dedicated efforts in place to protect these gentle giants. Learn about the conservation programs that aim to safeguard the nesting sites and educate visitors about the importance of turtle conservation. We'll also share tips on responsible turtle watching to ensure these majestic creatures are not disturbed.

## Whale and Dolphin Watching: Witness These Magnificent Marine Mammals in Their Natural Habitat

Mauritius isn't just a haven for coral and fish; it's also a playground for some of the ocean's largest and most captivating creatures. The waters surrounding the island are frequented by whales and dolphins, offering a thrilling opportunity to witness their awe-inspiring displays.

Magnificent Encounters: Join us on a journey to witness the grace and power of these marine mammals. From playful pods of dolphins to the majestic humpback whales, Mauritius provides a unique opportunity for marine enthusiasts to observe these creatures in their natural habitat. We'll provide insights into the best times and locations for your chances of encountering these magnificent animals.

Whether you're an experienced diver eager to explore the depths of the Indian Ocean, a snorkeler looking to glimpse the wonders of the coral reefs, or simply a nature lover hoping to witness the magic of sea turtles, Mauritius offers something extraordinary for every underwater explorer. No matter your level of expertise, the island's marine treasures are bound to leave an indelible impression on your journey through this aquatic wonderland.

## Discovering the Inner Beauty: Waterfalls and Hiking Trails

While the beaches are exquisite, Mauritius' interior is equally captivating. Verdant forests, dramatic gorges, and cascading waterfalls create a lush, natural playground for adventurers. We'll guide you through:

### Chamarel Waterfall: Marvel at the Mesmerizing Multi-Tiered Wonder

Nestled within the picturesque Chamarel region, the Chamarel Waterfall stands as a testament to nature's artistry. As you approach this natural masterpiece, the sound of rushing water grows louder, heightening your anticipation. Once you catch your first glimpse, you'll be captivated by the sight of a multi-tiered waterfall gracefully cascading down the lush, green slopes of the Black River Gorges. The contrast of the pure white water against the emerald backdrop is simply awe-inspiring.

A well-maintained pathway leads you through the verdant foliage, creating an enchanting journey to the base of the falls. Here, you'll feel the refreshing mist on your skin and hear the soothing roar of the water. It's an ideal spot for photography, meditation, or simply soaking in the tranquil ambiance of the surroundings.

## Black River Gorges National Park: A Hiker's Paradise

For those with a passion for hiking and a thirst for adventure, the Black River Gorges National Park beckons. This protected wilderness area spans over 65 square kilometers, offering a network of well-marked hiking trails that wind through its diverse landscapes. As you lace up your hiking boots, prepare to embark on an exploration of unparalleled beauty.

The park's trails cater to hikers of all levels, from leisurely strolls suitable for families to more challenging treks for experienced adventurers. Along the way, you'll encounter breathtaking viewpoints that overlook the rolling hills, dense forests, and deep gorges. Keep your eyes peeled for glimpses of the rare and endemic bird species that call this park home, including the Pink Pigeon and the Mauritius Kestrel.

## Tamarind Falls: A Hidden Gem in the Heart of the Island

Venture deep into the heart of Mauritius, and you'll discover the hidden gem known as Tamarind Falls, also called the "Sept Cascades" due to its seven distinct waterfalls. This natural wonder is tucked away in the lush highlands of the island, accessible through a scenic journey that takes you through small villages and dense forests.

Once you arrive, you'll be greeted by the melodious sound of water rushing over the rugged terrain. Tamarind Falls offers a unique hiking experience as you traverse challenging terrain to explore each of the cascades. The trek rewards you with the opportunity to swim in the pristine rock pools beneath the falls, providing a refreshing break from the hike. It's an adventure that combines exploration with rejuvenation.

In Mauritius, the interior landscape is an enchanting canvas of nature's finest works. Whether you're seeking leisurely nature walks or challenging treks, the island offers a variety of hiking experiences suitable for all levels of fitness. These natural wonders invite you to immerse yourself in the beauty and serenity of Mauritius' interior, a world waiting to be discovered.

# The Mystical Chamarel Colored Earths

Venture into the southwest of Mauritius, and you'll discover the otherworldly landscape known as the Chamarel Colored Earths.

Nestled in the heart of the captivating southwest region of Mauritius lies one of the island's most enigmatic natural wonders—the Chamarel Colored Earths. This extraordinary geological formation is a testament to nature's artistic prowess, and visiting it is like stepping onto another planet.

## *A Palette of Seven Distinct Colors*

What truly makes the Chamarel Colored Earths a must-see attraction is the remarkable array of colors that grace this unusual terrain. These naturally occurring sand dunes showcase a surreal blend of seven distinct hues, each with its own distinct shade and texture. As you gaze upon this kaleidoscope of colors, you'll be captivated by the shifting gradients, ranging from rich reds and earthy browns to striking purples and deep blues.

## *Unraveling the Geological Phenomena*

Behind this seemingly magical display of colors lies a fascinating geological explanation. The sands of Chamarel are comprised of volcanic ash and basaltic rocks, which have undergone intricate weathering processes over thousands of years. The iron and aluminum content in the soil oxidizes at different rates, leading to the diverse range of colors that you witness today. The Chamarel Colored Earths stand as a testament to the complex interplay of geological forces that have shaped this part of the island.

## *Witnessing the Colors at Their Most Vibrant*

To experience the Chamarel Colored Earths at their most vibrant, timing is everything. The colors tend to be most vivid during sunny days, particularly in the early morning or late afternoon when the sunlight creates a stunning contrast against the dunes. The midday sun can be harsh, slightly muting the colors, so plan your visit accordingly to maximize the visual impact of this natural wonder.

## *Exploring Nearby Attractions*

Your journey to Chamarel isn't limited to the Colored Earths alone. In the vicinity, you'll find other enticing attractions that enrich your visit:

- Chamarel Waterfall: Just a short distance from the Colored Earths, this waterfall plunges from a height of 100 meters into a lush gorge. The view is nothing short of breathtaking, and a viewing platform provides an excellent vantage point for photos.

- Rhumerie de Chamarel: After marveling at nature's artistry, you can savor some of the island's finest rum at the nearby Rhumerie de Chamarel. Take a guided tour of the distillery to learn about the rum-making process and enjoy tastings of their exquisite rum varieties.

Visiting Chamarel is an unforgettable journey into the heart of Mauritius' natural beauty and geological wonders. It's an experience that appeals to both the curious traveler and the nature enthusiast, leaving you with lasting memories of an island where magic seems to seep from the very earth itself.

## Underwater Waterfall Illusion at Le Morne

While exploring the iconic Le Morne Peninsula, you'll encounter a mesmerizing natural phenomenon: the underwater waterfall illusion.

Nestled along the southwestern coastline of Mauritius, the Le Morne Peninsula is famous for its stunning beauty and rich cultural history. But it's not just what's above the surface that makes this place remarkable; it's what lies beneath the waves that truly astounds.

This optical illusion occurs due to the interaction of underwater currents and the coral reef drop-off, creating the appearance of a cascading waterfall beneath the ocean's surface.

As you stand on the shoreline, gazing out at the ocean, you might notice a peculiar sight. It seems as though the water is flowing downward, just like a waterfall, right there in the depths of the sea. However, there's no actual waterfall here.

What you're witnessing is an astonishing natural illusion created by a confluence of factors.

At the heart of this optical spectacle is the unique underwater topography surrounding Le Morne Peninsula. The island's coral reef system, which fringes the peninsula, abruptly drops off into the deep ocean. This dramatic change in underwater terrain creates a sort of underwater 'cliff,' where the ocean floor suddenly plunges to considerable depths.

Here's how the magic happens: Ocean currents carrying sand and silt from the shallower lagoon areas get funneled toward this underwater cliff. When these currents meet the steep drop-off, they are forced downward and outward, creating a mesmerizing visual effect. The sand and silt are pushed down and away, giving the illusion of a cascading waterfall.

Dive or take a boat tour to witness this extraordinary sight up close and learn about the science behind this breathtaking natural wonder.

To truly appreciate this captivating phenomenon, adventurous travelers have the option to dive beneath the surface or embark on a boat tour. Diving allows you to descend into the depths and swim amidst the illusion, giving you a front-row seat to this surreal display. As you navigate through the currents and witness the sand flowing like water, you'll feel like you're in the midst of an enchanting underwater dreamscape.

For those who prefer to stay dry, boat tours are an excellent option. Knowledgeable guides on these tours provide insights into the science behind the underwater waterfall illusion, explaining how the interaction of currents and the unique underwater geography of the Le Morne Peninsula creates this optical wonder. They'll also share the cultural and historical significance of the area, including its connection to the island's history of marooned slaves and the struggle for freedom.

In either case, witnessing the underwater waterfall illusion at Le Morne is an unforgettable experience that combines the mysteries of nature with the thrill of exploration, leaving you with a profound appreciation for the wonders of the ocean.

## Ile aux Aigrettes: A Conservation Success Story

Nestled just off the southeastern coast of Mauritius, Ile aux Aigrettes is a small but extraordinary offshore island that beckons nature enthusiasts and conservationists alike. This pristine islet is a shining example of habitat restoration, where dedicated efforts have transformed it into a haven for native flora and fauna that were once on the brink of extinction.

### A Model of Habitat Restoration

Ile aux Aigrettes stands as a testament to the unwavering commitment of Mauritius to safeguard its unique ecosystems. Once overrun by invasive species and habitat degradation, this island has undergone an incredible transformation through decades of meticulous work. Conservationists have painstakingly removed invasive plants, restored native vegetation, and created a balanced, self-sustaining ecosystem.

## Discover the Unique Flora and Fauna

As you set foot on Ile aux Aigrettes, you'll step into a world teeming with remarkable biodiversity. Here, you'll have the chance to encounter flora and fauna found nowhere else on Earth. Keep an eye out for the enchanting Pink Pigeon, a rare and endemic bird species that has made a remarkable comeback thanks to conservation efforts on the island.

The island is also home to the ancient Aldabra giant tortoises, a species that once roamed freely across Mauritius but became critically endangered due to habitat loss and hunting. Witness these gentle giants as they leisurely graze amidst the lush vegetation, showcasing the success of the island's conservation initiatives.

## Efforts to Protect Endangered Species

Explore the behind-the-scenes work carried out by dedicated conservationists who monitor and protect the island's wildlife. Learn about the Pink Pigeon breeding programs and the meticulous care given to the giant tortoises. Understand the challenges faced in safeguarding these species and the ongoing research aimed at ensuring their survival.

## Eco-Friendly Practices

Ile aux Aigrettes goes beyond species conservation; it's also a shining example of eco-friendly practices. Discover how the island employs sustainable methods for waste management, energy production, and eco-tourism. Gain insights into how visitors can minimize their ecological footprint while exploring this fragile ecosystem.

### *Preserving Mauritius' Natural Heritage*

Ile aux Aigrettes is a beacon of hope in the realm of conservation. It showcases what can be achieved when dedicated individuals and communities come together to protect their natural heritage. As you explore this island, you'll not only witness the resurgence of endangered species but also be inspired by Mauritius' commitment to preserving its unique biodiversity for generations to come.

A visit to Ile aux Aigrettes is not just an exploration of a remote island; it's a journey into the heart of conservation and a celebration of the remarkable progress made in safeguarding Mauritius' natural treasures.

This chapter will open your eyes to the natural splendors of Mauritius, encouraging you to explore the island's diverse landscapes and experience its unspoiled beauty. Whether you're a beach lover, a marine enthusiast, or a nature explorer, Mauritius has something truly magical to offer.

# Chapter 8: Adventure Awaits

Mauritius, with its stunning landscapes and crystal-clear waters, is a playground for adventure seekers. In this chapter, we dive into the heart-pounding activities that will get your adrenaline pumping. Whether you're a water sports enthusiast, a nature lover, or an adventure junkie, Mauritius has something special in store for you.

## Water Sports and Activities: Snorkeling, Diving, and Surfing

### Mauritius' Submarine Wonderland

Beneath the turquoise waters that gently caress the shores of Mauritius lies a world of wonder and enchantment, a realm where reality merges with the surreal. Snorkeling and diving in Mauritius offer travelers an opportunity to explore a vibrant and diverse marine world that is truly unlike any other.

### *A Tapestry of Color and Life*

As you dip beneath the surface, you'll find yourself immersed in a living tapestry of color and life. Mauritius' coral reefs are a kaleidoscope of hues, with corals in every conceivable shade, from delicate pastels to vibrant neons. These corals provide a vital habitat for an astonishing array of marine species.

### Underwater Ballet

The waters surrounding Mauritius are a bustling metropolis of marine life. Schools of exotic fish dart gracefully among the corals, each species more colorful and captivating than the last. Keep your eyes peeled for parrotfish, clownfish, angelfish, and the majestic lionfish. With every stroke of your fins, you'll be treated to a mesmerizing underwater ballet.

### Graceful Sea Turtles

One of the most magical encounters you can have in Mauritius is with the island's gentle giants - sea turtles. These ancient creatures glide effortlessly through the water, their wise eyes regarding you with curiosity. Green turtles and hawksbill turtles are commonly spotted here, and if you're lucky, you might even witness them laying their eggs on the sandy beaches during nesting season.

### Dolphins at Play

Mauritius' waters are also home to playful pods of dolphins. Spinner dolphins, with their acrobatic spins and leaps, are known to frolic in the Indian Ocean. You can embark on dolphin-watching excursions, where you'll have the chance to witness these magnificent creatures in their natural habitat.

### The Best Spots for Exploration

To ensure you have an unforgettable underwater adventure, we've carefully curated a list of the best snorkeling and diving spots in Mauritius. Whether you're a novice or an experienced diver, there's a spot for you:

- Blue Bay Marine Park: Ideal for beginners, this park boasts crystal-clear waters, vibrant corals, and a diverse range of marine life. Snorkelers will find it especially enchanting.

- Trou aux Biches: Known for its shallow, calm waters, this spot is perfect for both snorkeling and beginner divers. You'll encounter colorful fish and abundant corals just a few strokes from the shore.

- Coin de Mire: For more experienced divers, this underwater haven offers thrilling drop-offs and caves to explore. Keep an eye out for reef sharks and barracudas.

- Flic en Flac: A popular diving spot on the west coast, it's famous for its diverse marine life, including seahorses, rays, and turtles.

- Île aux Cerfs: A snorkeler's paradise, this island is surrounded by shallow, clear waters filled with an abundance of fish species.

## Conquering the Waves: Surfing in Paradise

Mauritius is not just an island of tranquil beaches and underwater beauty; it's also a surfer's dream destination. With waves that cater to all skill levels, from beginners eager to catch their first ride to experts seeking the ultimate thrill, Mauritius offers an exceptional surfing experience.

### Riding the Indian Ocean's Swells

Surfing in Mauritius means riding the swells of the mighty Indian Ocean. The island's unique geography and position in the ocean make it an ideal destination for surfers of all backgrounds.

### The Best Surf Spots

Let's explore some of the best surf spots that Mauritius has to offer:

- Tamarin Bay: This legendary break is renowned for its consistent waves and is a favorite among both local and visiting surfers. It's particularly suited for experienced surfers looking for a challenge.

- One Eye, Le Morne: Famous for its powerful and hollow waves, One Eye is a paradise for experienced surfers and kite surfers. The backdrop of the iconic Le Morne Brabant mountain adds to the allure of this spot.

- Grande Riviere Noire: A perfect spot for beginners and longboarders, Grande Riviere Noire offers mellow waves and a relaxed atmosphere. It's an excellent place to take your first steps on a surfboard.

- Roches Noires: This spot caters to surfers of all levels and is known for its consistency. You'll find both left and right reef breaks here, making it a versatile choice.

- Baie du Cap: Ideal for beginners and intermediate surfers, Baie du Cap features a long sandy beach with gentle waves, providing the perfect setting to practice your skills.

## *Surfing Tips from Locals*

To make the most of your surfing adventure in Mauritius, consider seeking advice from local surfers. They know the ins and outs of the waves, currents, and hidden gems. You'll often find a tight-knit and welcoming surf community on the island.

## *Surf Schools and Rentals*

For those new to surfing or looking to improve their skills, Mauritius boasts numerous surf schools that offer lessons, equipment rentals, and experienced instructors. Whether you're a beginner or just looking to refine your technique, these schools will help you catch your first wave or ride it to perfection.

## *Surf's Up in Mauritius*

Surfing in Mauritius is not just a sport; it's an experience that connects you with the raw power of the ocean. Whether you're paddling out to catch your first wave or dropping into a barrel, the thrill is undeniable. And with its warm waters, consistent waves, and stunning backdrops, Mauritius truly is a surfer's paradise.

# Exploring National Parks and Wildlife Reserves

## Into the Wild: Mauritius' Ecological Treasures

Mauritius is a paradise not only for beach bums and water sports enthusiasts but also for nature lovers and eco-enthusiasts. Beyond its pristine coastlines, the island boasts an incredible wealth of ecological treasures, including lush forests, unique flora, and endemic fauna. In this section, we invite you to embark on a journey through Mauritius' national parks and wildlife reserves, offering a chance to witness rare and endangered species like the Mauritian kestrel and the giant Aldabra tortoise. Whether you're a hiker, bird-watcher, or simply someone looking to connect with nature, Mauritius has something remarkable in store for you.

## Black River Gorges National Park: A Hiker's Paradise

Nestled in the southwestern part of Mauritius lies the magnificent Black River Gorges National Park, a haven for hikers and nature enthusiasts alike. Covering an expansive 67.54 square kilometers, this park is a gem waiting to be discovered.

## *Exploring the Trails*

One of the park's standout features is its extensive network of hiking trails, ranging from leisurely strolls to challenging treks. As you venture deeper into the park, you'll be surrounded by lush, verdant forests teeming with an astonishing diversity of plant life, including many endemic species.

For an easy introduction, start with the Black River Gorges Visitors' Center, which offers informative exhibits about the park's flora and fauna. From here, you can set off on the self-guided Macchabee Trail, a gentle path leading to the impressive Alexandra Falls. If you prefer a more challenging adventure, the 11-kilometer Black River Peak Trail takes you to the highest point on the island, rewarding you with breathtaking panoramic views of the surrounding landscape.

## *Bird-Watching Paradise*

Black River Gorges National Park is a birder's paradise, home to a variety of avian species, including the endemic and endangered Mauritius kestrel. Bird-watchers can spot these remarkable raptors soaring in the clear skies while keeping an eye out for other endemic species like the pink pigeon and the Mauritius parakeet. The park's well-maintained trails offer excellent opportunities for bird-watching, so be sure to bring your binoculars and a keen eye.

### *Discovering Unique Flora*

Throughout your hike, you'll encounter Mauritius' unique flora, which includes rare and indigenous plant species. Keep an eye out for the famous ebony and tambalacoque trees, both of which are exclusive to the island and play crucial roles in the island's ecosystem.

### *Panoramic Viewpoints*

As you traverse the park's undulating terrain, you'll come across breathtaking panoramic viewpoints. These spots provide excellent opportunities to rest, take photographs, and immerse yourself in the natural beauty that surrounds you. From the Gorges Viewpoint, you can gaze out over the Black River Gorges and witness the majestic landscapes that make this park so renowned.

### *Guided Tours and Tips*

For those seeking more in-depth knowledge about the park, consider joining a guided eco-tour. Knowledgeable guides will lead you through the park, providing insights into its ecology, history, and conservation efforts. Additionally, it's advisable to wear comfortable hiking attire, sturdy shoes, and bring plenty of water and sunscreen to ensure a safe and enjoyable trek.

Exploring Black River Gorges National Park is a memorable and enriching experience. It allows you to connect with nature in a profound way, immersing yourself in the island's unique ecological wonders. So, lace up your hiking boots, grab your camera, and get ready to discover the enchanting beauty of Mauritius' wilderness.

## Adrenaline-Pumping Adventures: Zip-lining, Quad Biking, and More

**Soaring High: Zip-lining Over Treetops**

Mauritius beckons adventure enthusiasts with an opportunity to defy gravity and experience the island's breathtaking landscapes from a whole new angle. If you seek the thrill of flight, you're in for a treat with Mauritius' exhilarating zip-lining experiences.

Picture yourself suspended above the lush green canopies, rivers, and waterfalls of the island's interior. The feeling of wind rushing through your hair as you glide along steel cables high above the tropical foliage is nothing short of exhilarating. Imagine the sheer excitement as you take that first step off the platform and begin your journey through the treetops.

We understand that safety is a top priority when it comes to high-flying adventures like zip-lining. That's why we've done the research to guide you to the top zip-lining providers on the island. These experienced professionals prioritize safety while ensuring you have a thrilling adventure. From securing your harness to providing expert guidance, they'll make your zip-lining experience safe, memorable, and full of adrenaline.

## Off-Road Excitement: Quad Biking

For those who crave off-road excitement and want to explore the rugged side of Mauritius, quad biking is the way to go. This heart-pounding adventure takes you through terrains that most tourists never get to see.

As you hop on your quad bike, you'll traverse diverse landscapes, from vast sugar cane fields that stretch as far as the eye can see to volcanic terrains with dramatic rock formations. You'll even venture into dense forests, where the thrill of navigating challenging paths adds an extra layer of excitement.

Quad biking allows you to experience Mauritius from a unique perspective. It's not just about the destination; it's about the journey itself. The freedom to explore off the beaten path, soak in the island's natural beauty, and feel the rush of adrenaline as you conquer diverse terrains makes quad biking an unforgettable adventure.

Skydiving and Parasailing: Conquer the Skies

For the true thrill-seekers, Mauritius offers two ultimate sky-bound adventures: skydiving and parasailing.

Skydiving promises an unmatched adrenaline rush. Imagine the heart-pounding anticipation as you ascend to altitude in an aircraft, knowing that the moment you step out of that plane, you'll experience free-fall at its finest. As you plummet through the Mauritian skies, your senses will come alive, and your heart will race. Then, as your parachute opens, you'll be treated to breathtaking views of the island from a vantage point few will ever know.

If you're seeking a more relaxed aerial adventure with stunning coastal panoramas, parasailing is your ticket to conquering the skies. Suspended beneath a colorful parachute, you'll gently ascend into the air, allowing you to soak in Mauritius' magnificent coastline. It's a thrilling yet serene experience that provides a unique perspective of the island's natural beauty.

In this chapter, we've unveiled some of the most heart-pounding and awe-inspiring adventures that Mauritius has to offer. Whether you're soaring through the treetops, conquering rugged terrains on a quad bike, or defying gravity with skydiving and parasailing, Mauritius promises unforgettable moments of adrenaline and exhilaration.

# Chapter 9: Shopping and Souvenirs

Mauritius offers a vibrant shopping scene that caters to both shopaholics and those seeking unique souvenirs to commemorate their island adventure. In this chapter, we'll explore the diverse shopping opportunities, from local markets and handicrafts to finding authentic souvenirs while promoting sustainable shopping practices.

## Local Markets and Handicrafts

### Port Louis Central Market: A Burst of Color and Culture

**Address: Corderie St, Port Louis, Mauritius**

When you find yourself in Port Louis, Mauritius' vibrant capital, a visit to the Central Market is a must for any traveler. This bustling marketplace is a microcosm of Mauritian life, offering a sensory overload of sights, sounds, and flavors.

As you step into the Port Louis Central Market, you'll be greeted by a kaleidoscope of colors. Stalls are laden with fresh produce, creating a vivid mosaic of tropical fruits and vegetables that seem to glow with natural vibrancy. Take your time to explore the fruit and vegetable section; it's a chance to taste the island's exotic flavors, like lychee, jackfruit, and dragon fruit.

Beyond the produce, the market transforms into a treasure trove of handmade crafts and local street food. Craftsmen display their artistry in stalls filled with vibrant textiles, intricate jewelry, and wooden sculptures carved with painstaking detail. Whether you're looking for a unique souvenir or a gift for a loved one, the Central Market offers a diverse selection of options.

Don't forget to immerse yourself in the fragrant world of Mauritian spices. Vendors here peddle a spectrum of spices, from fiery chili powders to fragrant vanilla pods, each with its unique story and culinary purpose.

And as you explore, your senses will lead you to the heart of the market, where the aroma of local street food wafts through the air. From samosas to dholl puri (a delicious Mauritian street food made of flatbreads filled with spiced lentils), you can savor the island's culinary delights right here. Grab a bite, engage in friendly banter with the locals, and absorb the lively atmosphere.

**Flacq Market: Where Mauritian Culture Thrives**

**Address: Flacq, Mauritius**

Venturing to the east of the island, you'll discover the Flacq Market, the largest open-air market in Mauritius. This vibrant marketplace is more than just a shopping destination; it's a cultural experience that allows you to immerse yourself in the heart and soul of Mauritius.

The Flacq Market is a kaleidoscope of colors and traditions. Stalls teem with a rich variety of items, from clothing and textiles to jewelry and artisanal crafts. Local artists and craftsmen proudly display their creations, often with intricate patterns and designs that reflect the island's diverse heritage.

As you stroll through the market, you'll find it impossible not to be captivated by the lively atmosphere. The sounds of vendors haggling and shoppers bargaining create a symphony of Mauritian life. Take your time to engage with the vendors, learn about the stories behind their crafts, and appreciate the cultural richness that the market embodies.

Whether you're looking for traditional Mauritian clothing, unique jewelry pieces, or just want to soak in the local culture, a visit to the Flacq Market is an experience that will leave you with lasting memories of Mauritius.

## Quatre Bornes Market: The City of Flowers and More

### Address: Quatre Bornes, Mauritius

Every Sunday, Quatre Bornes, known as the "City of Flowers," transforms into a vibrant marketplace that offers much more than just blooms. It's an enchanting place to spend your day, filled with an array of delights for shoppers and explorers alike.

Start your visit by taking in the colorful spectacle of fresh flowers. The market overflows with bouquets, arrangements, and individual blossoms, each a testament to the island's natural beauty. Whether you're in search of a fragrant gift or simply want to immerse yourself in a sea of blooms, Quatre Bornes Market delivers.

Beyond the floral wonders, you'll discover a diverse array of goods. Clothing stalls showcase a mix of traditional and modern styles, making it a great place to shop for garments with a Mauritian touch. Textiles, accessories, and locally crafted souvenirs are also abundant, giving you ample opportunities to find that special keepsake.

For those interested in Mauritius' unique natural history, keep an eye out for miniature model dodos. These flightless birds, native to Mauritius, are now extinct but live on as charming souvenirs. These model dodos are a fitting symbol of your journey through the "City of Flowers."

Quatre Bornes Market isn't just about shopping; it's about embracing the local culture and enjoying a leisurely Sunday surrounded by the warmth of Mauritian hospitality.

**Handicraft Villages: Artistry at Its Finest**

**Various Locations Across the Island**

Throughout Mauritius, you'll stumble upon enchanting handicraft villages that offer an authentic glimpse into the island's creative soul. These villages are where local artisans transform raw materials into exquisite items, showcasing their skills and preserving the island's artistic heritage.

As you explore these charming villages, you'll have the unique opportunity to watch skilled craftsmen and craftswomen at work. Witness potters shape clay into intricate forms, weavers create vibrant textiles, and woodcarvers bring life to their creations with deft strokes of their tools. It's an educational and immersive experience that provides a deeper appreciation for the craftsmanship behind the souvenirs you'll encounter.

Among the items crafted in these villages, you'll find pottery adorned with traditional Mauritian patterns, textiles showcasing vibrant colors and intricate designs, and wooden sculptures that capture the essence of the island's flora and fauna.

By purchasing from these handicraft villages, you not only acquire authentic, handmade souvenirs but also directly support local artisans and their communities. It's a meaningful way to bring a piece of Mauritius' creative spirit home with you while contributing to the preservation of its cultural heritage.

## Where to Find Authentic Souvenirs

### L'Aventure du Sucre Boutique

**Location**: L'Aventure du Sucre museum, Beau Plan, Pamplemousses

Nestled within the captivating L'Aventure du Sucre museum in the picturesque village of Pamplemousses, the L'Aventure du Sucre Boutique is a delightful destination for those with a sweet tooth and an appreciation for Mauritius' sugar heritage. This charming boutique invites visitors to immerse themselves in the island's centuries-old sugar industry while offering an array of delectable sugar-related products.

As you step into this enticing space, you're greeted by the tantalizing aroma of sugary delights. Here, you can explore an extensive collection of flavored sugars, each carefully crafted to capture the essence of the island. Sample the exotic flavors of tropical fruits like mango and pineapple infused into fine sugar crystals, and select your favorites to take home as a sweet reminder of your Mauritius journey.

For those seeking something a bit stronger, the boutique offers an impressive selection of locally produced rum. Mauritius is renowned for its rum-making tradition, and you'll find a variety of aged and spiced rums, each with a unique flavor profile. Whether you're a connoisseur or a novice, the knowledgeable staff can guide you in choosing the perfect bottle to commemorate your visit.

One of the most captivating aspects of the L'Aventure du Sucre Boutique is its display of exquisite sugar sculptures. These intricate works of art are crafted by skilled sugar artisans, showcasing the island's rich history through sugar-based creations. From miniature sugar dodos to elaborate sculptures depicting key moments in Mauritius' past, these pieces are both visually stunning and culturally significant.

As you explore the boutique, you'll not only find delightful souvenirs but also gain a deeper appreciation for the integral role sugar has played in shaping the identity of Mauritius. It's a sensory journey that combines history, culture, and the pleasures of the palate, making it a must-visit destination for anyone exploring the island's heritage.

**Caudan Waterfront**

**Location**: Caudan Waterfront, Port Louis

In the heart of the bustling capital city, Port Louis, lies the Caudan Waterfront, a premier shopping and entertainment complex that beckons to travelers and locals alike. This vibrant destination is not only a shopper's paradise but also a hub of culture and leisure.

Caudan Waterfront's allure is immediately apparent as you stroll along its picturesque waterfront promenade, with stunning views of the harbor and the ocean beyond. The complex houses a diverse array of shops, making it an ideal location to pick up high-quality souvenirs and gifts.

For fashion enthusiasts, the designer clothing boutiques offer a chance to indulge in the latest styles and trends. From international brands to locally designed fashion, you'll find a wide selection to suit every taste. Jewelry stores glisten with exquisite pieces, some crafted with locally sourced gemstones, making for elegant keepsakes.

Local craftspeople and artisans also have a presence at Caudan Waterfront. Their stalls and shops showcase a rich tapestry of Mauritian craftsmanship, offering an array of handmade items, including intricate textiles, hand-carved wooden artifacts, and vibrant paintings that capture the island's natural beauty.

As you explore the complex, you'll discover charming cafes and restaurants where you can take a break and savor Mauritian cuisine or international dishes while enjoying the lively atmosphere. With its mix of shopping, dining, and cultural experiences, Caudan Waterfront embodies the dynamic spirit of Port Louis and provides a delightful opportunity to shop for treasures that reflect the essence of Mauritius.

**Le Craft Market**

**Location**: Grand Baie, Mauritius

Nestled in the heart of Grand Baie, Le Craft Market is a hidden gem for travelers seeking authentic and locally made souvenirs. This bustling market is a testament to Mauritius' rich artisanal traditions and is a treasure trove of unique gifts and keepsakes.

As you wander through the market's vibrant stalls, you'll be greeted by a kaleidoscope of colors and textures. Mauritius' multicultural heritage is on full display here, with artisans hailing from diverse backgrounds crafting an array of goods that reflect the island's identity.

Textiles take center stage at Le Craft Market. You'll find beautifully woven fabrics, vibrant batik clothing, and intricately embroidered linens that showcase the island's cultural diversity. Whether you're looking for a sarong to wear on the beach or a decorative textile for your home, you're sure to find something that catches your eye.

Woodworking is another prominent craft at the market. Artisans skillfully carve wooden masks, figurines, and home decor items that often feature intricate detailing and traditional motifs. These pieces not only make for captivating souvenirs but also carry a piece of Mauritian culture with them.

The market is also a fantastic place to explore the world of local art. Paintings, sculptures, and pottery created by Mauritian artists adorn the stalls, offering a glimpse into the island's thriving art scene. You may even have the opportunity to meet the artists themselves and gain insight into their creative processes.

What sets Le Craft Market apart is the warm and welcoming atmosphere. The artisans take pride in sharing their craft and culture with visitors, making each shopping experience a memorable and enriching one. So, whether you're in search of a vibrant textile, an intricately carved wooden item, or a piece of Mauritian art, Le Craft Market in Grand Baie is the place to be for a truly authentic shopping adventure.

## Sustainable Shopping: Supporting Local Artisans

### Fair Trade Shops: Empowering Local Artisans

Mauritius is home to a wealth of talented artisans who produce exquisite handicrafts and unique souvenirs. When you're exploring the island and looking for meaningful keepsakes, consider seeking out fair trade shops and cooperatives. These establishments play a vital role in supporting the livelihoods of local craftsmen and women while promoting sustainable practices.

Fair trade shops in Mauritius are committed to ensuring that artisans receive fair wages for their work. This means that the creators behind the beautiful crafts you encounter are paid a reasonable and equitable income for their efforts. This fair compensation helps improve their quality of life, supports their families, and enables them to continue practicing their traditional crafts with pride and dignity.

Furthermore, these fair trade outlets often prioritize sustainable working conditions. This includes safe and ethical workspaces, access to necessary resources, and respect for the environment. When you purchase from these shops, you can be confident that your souvenirs are not only beautiful but also ethically produced.

By choosing to shop at fair trade establishments, you actively contribute to the empowerment of Mauritius' talented artisans. Your support enables them to preserve their craft traditions and pass them on to future generations. It also promotes economic sustainability within local communities, helping to create a brighter future for all involved.

**Community Markets: Connecting with Local Artisans**

While exploring Mauritius, keep an eye out for community markets and events where artisans directly showcase their creations. These markets provide a unique opportunity for you to connect with the people behind the products and learn about their craft traditions.

When you purchase from these markets, your money goes directly to the individuals who created the items you're buying. This direct connection ensures that artisans receive the full value of their work, allowing them to continue practicing and preserving their unique skills.

Community markets often offer a wide variety of handcrafted goods, from intricately woven textiles to beautifully carved wooden sculptures. You'll also find unique, one-of-a-kind pieces that make for exceptional souvenirs and gifts.

By supporting community markets, you play a direct role in supporting the local economy. Your purchases contribute to the economic well-being of the artisans and their families, helping to uplift the communities you visit. Additionally, engaging with artisans at these markets provides a rich cultural exchange, allowing you to gain insights into the traditions, stories, and inspirations behind their creations.

In essence, whether you choose to shop at fair trade shops or explore community markets, your conscientious purchases make a positive impact on Mauritius' artisanal communities. You not only bring home beautiful and meaningful souvenirs but also contribute to the preservation of cultural heritage and the sustainable development of the island.

By exploring Mauritius' local markets, discovering authentic souvenirs, and embracing sustainable shopping practices, you not only bring home cherished mementos but also contribute to the preservation of the island's rich cultural heritage and environment. Happy shopping!

# Chapter 10: Travel Itineraries

## Family friendly itinerary

Mauritius, often dubbed the "Paradise Island," is a dream destination for travelers of all kinds, and families are no exception. This picturesque island in the Indian Ocean offers a perfect blend of natural beauty, adventure, and relaxation, making it an ideal place for a family vacation. From stunning beaches to thrilling activities and cultural experiences, Mauritius has something for everyone. In this guide, we'll explore family-friendly itineraries to help you make the most of your trip to this tropical paradise.

Day 1: Arrival in Paradise

Morning:

- Arrival at Sir Seewoosagur Ramgoolam International Airport: As you step off the plane, the warm tropical breeze welcomes you to Mauritius. Sir Seewoosagur Ramgoolam International Airport is the main gateway to the island and offers a glimpse of the friendly atmosphere you'll encounter throughout your stay.

- Check into your family-friendly accommodation: Your journey begins with a seamless check-in process at your carefully selected family-friendly resort or hotel. The island boasts a range of accommodations catering to families, ensuring a comfortable and memorable stay.

- Spend some leisure time exploring the resort or beach: After settling into your room, take a moment to explore your resort's lush surroundings. Stroll through beautifully landscaped gardens, lounge by the pool, or take a short walk to the beach. This time allows you to unwind and adjust to the island's relaxed pace.

Afternoon:

- Enjoy a welcome lunch with local flavors at the resort: Delight your taste buds with a welcome lunch at your resort's restaurant. Mauritius is renowned for its diverse cuisine, which blends Creole, Indian, Chinese, and French influences. Savor the first of many culinary adventures during your stay.

- Familiarize yourself with the resort's amenities, including the pool and kids' club: After lunch, it's time for family-friendly fun. Most resorts in Mauritius offer fantastic amenities like pools with waterslides, supervised kids' clubs, and recreational activities for all ages. Let the children explore and make new friends while you relax.

- Take a relaxing stroll along the beach and watch the sunset: As the afternoon sun mellows, take a leisurely walk along the pristine beach. Mauritius is famous for its stunning sunsets, and this is your chance to witness one of nature's most beautiful spectacles. Enjoy quality family time as you build anticipation for the adventures ahead.

Day 2: Beach Day at Belle Mare

Morning:

- After a hearty breakfast at your resort, head to Belle Mare Beach on the east coast: Fuel up with a sumptuous breakfast spread at your resort, where you can savor both international and local breakfast delights. Then, pack your beach essentials and head to Belle Mare Beach, located on the island's serene east coast.

- Set up a beach spot with umbrellas and beach toys for the kids: Make yourselves comfortable on the soft, powdery sands of Belle Mare Beach. Set up beach umbrellas to create a shady oasis, and let the kids dive into a treasure chest of beach toys, ready for endless sandcastle building and beachcombing adventures.

- Explore the clear blue waters, build sandcastles, or simply relax under the sun: Whether your family prefers to take refreshing dips in the calm, crystal-clear waters, construct intricate sandcastles, or simply soak up the sun while the kids play, Belle Mare Beach offers a quintessential tropical beach experience.

Afternoon:

- Have a picnic lunch on the beach: For lunch, relish a beachfront picnic prepared with a variety of local delicacies and international favorites. Share stories, laugh, and make cherished memories while the waves gently lap the shore.

- Try some water sports like paddleboarding or glass-bottom boat rides: In the afternoon, introduce some adventure into your beach day. Belle Mare offers an array of water sports, from paddleboarding to glass-bottom boat rides. These activities cater to different skill levels and are perfect for family bonding.

- Return to your resort in the late afternoon and enjoy family time by the pool: As the sun begins to set, head back to your resort and rejuvenate at the pool. Let the kids splash around, and perhaps, indulge in refreshing cocktails while sharing stories of your beach escapades. The evening promises a relaxing atmosphere to unwind.

Day 3: Exploring Port Louis

Morning:

- After breakfast, take a day trip to the capital city, Port Louis: Start your day with a hearty breakfast at your resort. Then, embark on an exciting day trip to the bustling capital city of Port Louis. It's a chance for your family to dive into the island's history and culture.

- Visit the Aapravasi Ghat, a UNESCO World Heritage Site, to learn about the island's history: Begin your cultural journey at the Aapravasi Ghat, a UNESCO World Heritage Site. Here, you'll gain insights into the island's history, particularly its role in the indentured labor system during the 19th century.

- Explore the colorful Central Market and pick up some souvenirs: Immerse yourselves in the vibrant atmosphere of Port Louis' Central Market. The market is a sensory delight with stalls overflowing with exotic spices, fresh produce, local handicrafts, and souvenirs. It's the ideal place to pick up unique gifts and keepsakes.

Afternoon:

- Have a family-friendly lunch at a local restaurant: Enjoy a traditional Mauritian lunch at a local restaurant. Try dishes like dholl puri (a stuffed flatbread) or roti chaud (warm flatbread) with a variety of fillings, providing a taste of the island's diverse culinary heritage.

- Visit the Blue Penny Museum to see rare stamps and historical artifacts: Dive deeper into Mauritius' history at the Blue Penny Museum. Marvel at rare stamps, historical artifacts, and exhibits that recount the island's colonial past and its journey to independence.

- Take a stroll in the Caudan Waterfront, a shopping and entertainment complex: Conclude your day in Port Louis with a leisurely stroll along the picturesque Caudan Waterfront. It's a hub of shopping, dining, and entertainment, making it an ideal place for a family evening out.

Day 4: Adventure Day at Casela Nature Parks

Morning:

- Head to Casela Nature Parks for a day of adventure: Prepare for a day filled with thrills as you head to Casela Nature Parks. This adventure park offers a wide range of activities suitable for various age groups, promising unforgettable family moments.

- Participate in activities like ziplining, quad biking, and walking with lions (for older children): Choose from an array of exhilarating adventures, including ziplining through the treetops, exploring off-road trails on quad bikes, and even the unique opportunity for older children to walk alongside majestic lions under expert guidance.

- Enjoy a picnic lunch in the park: Refuel with a picnic lunch amidst the natural beauty of Casela. The park provides designated picnic spots where you can savor a delicious meal while surrounded by the island's breathtaking scenery.

Afternoon:

- Explore the park's animal sanctuary and see various species: After your adrenaline-pumping morning, switch gears and explore the park's animal sanctuary. Encounter a variety of animals, including deer, zebras, and giant tortoises, which are sure to captivate the entire family.

- Let the kids enjoy the petting farm and meet some friendly animals: For the little ones, the petting farm is a highlight. Here, children can get up close and personal with gentle farm animals, creating cherished memories of their time in Mauritius.

- Return to your resort and unwind in the evening: After a day of adventure, return to your resort in the late afternoon. It's time to unwind and relax, perhaps with a soothing swim in the pool or a peaceful walk on the beach.

## Day 5: Island Exploration - Ile aux Cerfs

Morning:

- Catch an early boat to Ile aux Cerfs, a beautiful island off the east coast: Begin your day with an early adventure by boarding a boat to Ile aux Cerfs, a stunning island situated off the east coast of Mauritius. The short boat ride sets the stage for an unforgettable day.

- Spend the morning on the pristine beaches, and swim in the crystal-clear waters: Arriving on Ile aux Cerfs is like stepping into a postcard. The island boasts pristine white-sand beaches and crystal-clear waters. Spend your morning building sandcastles, playing beach volleyball, or swimming in the inviting lagoon.

- Snorkel around the coral reefs and see colorful marine life: Explore the vibrant underwater world by snorkeling around the coral reefs. Mauritius' marine life is teeming with colorful fish and coral formations, making it an excellent opportunity for the whole family to discover the beauty beneath the waves.

Afternoon:

- Have a beachside lunch with barbecue seafood and local dishes: As the sun climbs higher in the sky, savor a delicious beachside barbecue lunch. Taste fresh seafood, grilled to perfection, and savor local dishes that reflect the island's culinary richness.

- Enjoy water sports like parasailing or banana boat rides: In the afternoon, get your adrenaline pumping with exciting water sports. Try parasailing for panoramic views of the island or enjoy the thrill of a banana boat ride, an experience both kids and adults will cherish.

- Return to your resort with sun-kissed skin and happy memories: As the day winds down, board the boat back to the mainland. The sunsets over the Indian Ocean are nothing short of spectacular. Return to your resort with sun-kissed skin and hearts full of happy memories.

Day 6: Cultural Immersion in Mahebourg

Morning:

- Drive to Mahebourg on the southern coast: After breakfast, embark on a scenic drive to Mahebourg, a charming town on the southern coast of Mauritius. Mahebourg offers a glimpse into the island's history and culture.

- Visit the National History Museum to learn about Mauritius' past: Start your cultural immersion by visiting the National History Museum, housed in a historic building. Here, you'll delve into Mauritius' past, from its colonial history to its struggle for independence.

- Explore Mahebourg Waterfront and enjoy views of the bay: Stroll along the Mahebourg Waterfront, where you can enjoy picturesque views of the bay, watch the local fishing boats, and soak in the town's serene atmosphere.

Afternoon:

- Savor a Creole lunch at a local restaurant: Treat your taste buds to a Creole lunch at a local restaurant in Mahebourg. Creole cuisine is known for its aromatic spices and flavors, creating a delightful dining experience.

- Visit the iconic Mahebourg Market, where you can shop for handmade crafts and spices: Spend the afternoon browsing the Mahebourg Market, where you'll find handmade crafts, vibrant textiles, and an array of spices. It's an ideal place to pick up unique souvenirs.

- Return to your resort for an evening of relaxation: After a day of cultural exploration, return to your resort for a peaceful evening. Enjoy the amenities, indulge in a spa treatment, or simply unwind by the pool.

Day 7: Nature and Wildlife at Black River Gorges National Park

Morning:

- After breakfast, head to Black River Gorges National Park: Kick off your day with a journey to Black River Gorges National Park, a sanctuary for nature enthusiasts. The park is known for its lush forests and stunning viewpoints.

- Embark on a family-friendly hike through lush forests and enjoy the stunning viewpoints: Choose a family-friendly hiking trail and venture into the heart of the park. Along the way, you'll encounter unique flora and fauna, with viewpoints offering panoramic vistas of the island's interior.

- Keep an eye out for unique flora and fauna: Black River Gorges National Park is home to many endemic species, including rare birds and plants. Encourage the kids to be on the lookout for these remarkable natural treasures.

Afternoon:

- Have a picnic lunch amidst nature: Find a picturesque spot within the park for a family picnic. Surrounded by the sights and sounds of nature, enjoy a peaceful lunch amidst the lush greenery.

- Visit the Gorges Viewpoint to see the Seven Colored Earths of Chamarel: After lunch, make your way to the Gorges Viewpoint, which offers a mesmerizing view of the Seven Colored Earths of Chamarel. This geological wonder is a must-see on the island.

- Return to your resort for a relaxing evening and perhaps a spa treatment for the adults: As the day concludes, return to your resort, where you can unwind with a soothing spa treatment for the adults. Let the children enjoy the resort's amenities or perhaps partake in some evening entertainment.

Day 8: Farewell to Mauritius

Morning:

- Enjoy your last breakfast in Mauritius: Savor your final breakfast in this tropical paradise. Relish the delicious spread at your resort, cherishing the flavors that have become familiar throughout your stay.

- Spend some quality time at the resort's beach or pool: Before check-out, make the most of your remaining time at the resort. Whether it's a leisurely morning walk on the beach or a refreshing swim in the pool, soak in the serene atmosphere.

- Check-out from your accommodation: As check-out time approaches, pack your belongings and bid farewell to your temporary island home. The staff will assist with the check-out process and can arrange airport transfers for your convenience.

Afternoon:

- Depending on your flight time, explore any last-minute shopping or relax at a beachfront cafe: If your flight departs in the afternoon or evening, take advantage of any remaining hours by exploring local shops for last-minute souvenirs or enjoying a relaxing lunch at a beachfront café.

- Head to the airport for your departure, bidding farewell to this enchanting island: When it's time to depart, make your way to Sir Seewoosagur Ramgoolam International Airport. As you board your flight, take with you the memories of an incredible family adventure in Mauritius.

Mauritius offers an array of family-friendly activities, ensuring that every member of the family, from kids to grandparents, can create lasting memories together. Whether you're exploring its natural wonders, immersing in its rich culture, or enjoying thrilling adventures, Mauritius truly is a paradise for families seeking a tropical getaway.

## 5-day travel Itinerary

Are you planning a trip to the stunning island of Mauritius? This 5-day travel itinerary will help you make the most of your visit, ensuring you experience the diverse range of activities, natural beauty, and cultural treasures this Indian Ocean paradise has to offer.

Day 1: Arrival and Acclimatization

Morning

- Arrive at Sir Seewoosagur Ramgoolam International Airport: Your adventure begins the moment you step off the plane and into this tropical paradise. The Sir Seewoosagur Ramgoolam International Airport, located in Plaine Magnien, is the gateway to Mauritius. As you disembark, you'll feel the warm, balmy air that's a hallmark of this island nation.

- Check-in to your chosen accommodation: Mauritius offers a diverse range of accommodation options to suit every traveler's preferences. Whether you've opted for a luxurious beachfront resort with panoramic ocean views, a cozy guesthouse nestled in lush tropical gardens, or a budget-friendly hotel with easy access to local attractions, your chosen lodging will likely offer a warm welcome and a taste of Mauritian hospitality.

Afternoon

- Spend your first day relaxing on one of Mauritius' world-famous beaches: After settling into your accommodation, it's time to experience one of the island's greatest treasures – its stunning beaches. You have several exceptional options to choose from, each with its unique charm. Grand Baie offers a lively atmosphere with a variety of water sports, shopping, and dining options. Flic en Flac boasts a more tranquil setting with a long stretch of pristine beach, perfect for sunbathing and swimming. Trou aux Biches is known for its gentle, crystal-clear waters, ideal for snorkeling and leisurely strolls along the shoreline.

- Take a dip in the crystal-clear waters and work on your tan: The turquoise waters that lap the shores of Mauritius are invitingly warm, making them perfect for a refreshing swim. Float on your back and let the gentle waves carry away your cares, or grab a snorkel and explore the colorful underwater world.

- Enjoy a leisurely beachfront lunch: After working up an appetite in the sun and sea, savor a delicious Mauritian meal at one of the local beachfront restaurants. Sample fresh seafood, tropical salads, and sip on exotic cocktails as you dine with the sound of the ocean in the background.

Evening

- Explore the vibrant nightlife of Grand Baie: As the sun begins to dip below the horizon, Grand Baie comes to life. Known for its lively nightlife scene, this area boasts numerous bars, clubs, and live music venues. Whether you're in the mood for dancing the night away or simply sipping cocktails under the stars, Grand Baie has something for everyone.

- Try some local dishes at a beachfront restaurant: Mauritian cuisine is a delightful fusion of flavors influenced by Indian, African, Chinese, and French culinary traditions. Taste local specialties like "boulettes," "dholl puri," or "rougaille" at a beachfront restaurant. These dishes provide a perfect introduction to the island's rich gastronomic heritage.

- Return to your accommodation for a well-deserved rest: After a day filled with travel and exploration, return to your comfortable lodgings for a restful night's sleep. You'll need your energy for the adventures that lie ahead.

Day 1 sets the tone for your Mauritius journey, introducing you to the island's natural beauty, inviting beaches, and vibrant culture. It's a day of relaxation and acclimatization, ensuring you're fully prepared for the adventures that await.

Day 2: Discovering Port Louis and Culture

Morning

- Start your day early and head to the capital city, Port Louis: Rise with the sun and set out for the heart of Mauritius, the bustling capital city of Port Louis. This city is a vibrant blend of cultures, history, and modernity.

- Visit the Caudan Waterfront: Begin your exploration at the Caudan Waterfront, a bustling shopping and entertainment complex located along the picturesque harbor. Take your time to wander through the shops, boutiques, and craft markets. Enjoy a coffee or tea at

one of the cafés, and relish the view of the boats bobbing in the harbor.
- Walk to the nearby Aapravasi Ghat: Just a short walk from the Caudan Waterfront, you'll find the Aapravasi Ghat, a UNESCO World Heritage site. This historical site holds deep significance as it was once the immigration depot for indentured laborers who arrived in Mauritius from India, bringing with them a rich cultural tapestry that still influences the island today.

Afternoon

- Discover the bustling Central Market: Make your way to the Central Market, locally known as the Port Louis Bazaar. Here, you'll be immersed in the sights, sounds, and flavors of local culture. Shop for spices, textiles, jewelry, and handcrafted souvenirs. The market is a sensory delight, with the aroma of spices and street food filling the air.

- Enjoy a traditional Creole lunch: Within the Central Market and its surrounding streets, you'll find numerous eateries offering authentic Mauritian dishes. Sample "dholl puri," a delicious street food favorite, or indulge in a traditional Creole meal featuring curries, chutneys, and rice.

Evening

- Explore the historical and cultural side of Port Louis: In the evening, delve into the history and culture of Port Louis. Visit the Blue Penny Museum, where you can view the world-famous Blue and Red Penny postage stamps, among other historical artifacts. Then, take a stroll to the nearby Champs de Mars

Racecourse, one of the oldest horse racing tracks in the Southern Hemisphere, and enjoy the lively atmosphere of a race evening.
- Savor an evening meal at a waterfront restaurant: As the night sky begins to twinkle with stars, dine at a waterfront restaurant in Port Louis. Enjoy seafood specialties or international cuisine while taking in breathtaking views of the city lights reflected on the harbor.

Day 2 immerses you in the vibrant culture and history of Mauritius, with visits to important landmarks and markets in Port Louis. It's a day of discovery, where you'll gain insight into the island's past and present, and savor the flavors of its cuisine. As you return to your accommodation in the evening, you'll carry with you the memories of a day well-spent in the capital city.

Day 3: Nature and Adventure

Morning

- Set off for an adventure-packed day in the Black River Gorges National Park: Leave the city behind and venture into the heart of nature at the Black River Gorges National Park. This protected area is a haven for nature enthusiasts, with its lush forests, diverse wildlife, and pristine hiking trails.

- Hike one of the park's well-marked trails: Lace up your hiking boots and choose from a variety of trails that cater to different fitness levels. The Black River Peak trail leads to the island's highest point, offering breathtaking panoramic views. Alternatively, opt for the Macchabee-Bel Ombre trail to explore the park's interior and discover unique plant and bird species.

- Keep an eye out for the park's unique flora and fauna: As you hike through the park, be on the lookout for Mauritius's rare and endemic wildlife. You might catch a glimpse of the pink pigeon, echo parakeet, or Mauritian flying fox, all of which are found nowhere else in the world.

Afternoon

- Continue your nature exploration by visiting Chamarel: After a morning of hiking, head to the village of Chamarel, known for its natural wonders. The highlight is undoubtedly the Seven Colored Earths, a geological phenomenon featuring sand dunes with seven distinct colors, caused by the varying mineral content in the soil.

- Enjoy lunch at a local restaurant surrounded by lush greenery: Chamarel offers several charming restaurants where you can savor Mauritian cuisine in a tranquil setting. Take your time to relish your meal amidst the stunning natural surroundings.

Evening

- Head back to your accommodation: After an active day exploring nature and discovering geological marvels, return to your accommodation to relax and unwind. This evening is perfect for enjoying a leisurely dinner at your lodging or exploring the local dining options nearby.

Day 3 is all about immersing yourself in the natural beauty of Mauritius. From hiking through lush forests to marveling at the unique geological features of Chamarel, you'll have a deeper appreciation for the island's biodiversity and stunning landscapes by the end of the day.

Now, let's move on to Day 4.

Day 4: Coastal Wonders and Water Activities

Morning

- Explore the picturesque village of Trou d'Eau Douce: Begin your day with a visit to the charming coastal village of Trou d'Eau Douce on the east coast of Mauritius. This quaint village exudes a laid-back ambiance and is the gateway to some exciting adventures.

- Take a boat trip to Ile aux Cerfs: From Trou d'Eau Douce, embark on a boat trip to Ile aux Cerfs, an iconic island known for its pristine white sandy beaches, crystal-clear waters, and a plethora of water sports activities.

Afternoon

- Indulge in a range of water activities: Ile aux Cerfs offers an array of water sports and activities to satisfy adventure seekers. Whether you're a fan of snorkeling, parasailing, jet-skiing, or simply want to relax on the beach, this island paradise has it all.

- Enjoy a beachfront barbecue lunch on the island: As the sun climbs high in the sky, savor a delicious beachfront barbecue lunch prepared by local chefs. Feast on grilled seafood, tropical fruits, and refreshing beverages as you take in the stunning surroundings.

Evening

- Return to the mainland: After an exhilarating day on Ile aux Cerfs, make your way back to the mainland in the late afternoon.

- Visit the iconic Belle Mare Plage for a breathtaking sunset: In the evening, head to the renowned Belle Mare Plage, a stunning stretch of coastline famous for its golden sands and turquoise waters. As the sun dips below the horizon, you'll be treated to a magical sunset, painting the sky with hues of orange, pink, and purple.

- Head back to your accommodation to freshen up before dinner: After witnessing the sunset at Belle Mare Plage, return to your accommodation to unwind and prepare for a delightful evening ahead.

Day 4 is a day of coastal exploration and water-based activities, offering the perfect balance between adventure and relaxation. From the picturesque Trou d'Eau Douce to the captivating beauty of Ile aux Cerfs and the mesmerizing sunset at Belle Mare Plage, this day will leave you with unforgettable memories of Mauritius.

Day 5: Culture, History, and Departure

Morning

- Visit the Domaine de l'Etoile: Begin your day with a visit to the Domaine de l'Etoile, a private nature reserve that offers a unique and immersive experience. Located in the heart of Mauritius, this reserve is a haven for adventure enthusiasts.

- Enjoy a quad bike or horseback ride: Explore the diverse landscapes of the Domaine de l'Etoile on a thrilling quad bike adventure or a leisurely horseback ride. Wind your way through lush forests, open plains, and scenic trails, getting a closer look at the island's natural beauty.

- Explore the reserve's cultural village: After your outdoor adventure, take time to discover the cultural village within the reserve. Here, you can learn about the history, traditions, and cultural heritage of Mauritius through interactive displays and engaging experiences.

Afternoon

- Enjoy a final meal in Mauritius at a local restaurant: Before bidding farewell to the island, treat yourself to a memorable meal at a local restaurant. Savor your favorite Mauritian dishes one last time, whether it's a hearty curry, flavorful street food, or a tropical fruit feast.

- Depending on your departure time: If your flight allows for it, you might have a few hours left to engage in some last-minute activities. Consider some shopping for souvenirs or enjoying a final stroll along the beach to soak up the sun and sea one more time.

Evening

- Check out from your accommodation: As the day comes to a close, it's time to check out from your chosen accommodation. Make sure you have all your belongings and souvenirs gathered.

- Head to the airport for your departure: Arrange for transportation to Sir Seewoosagur Ramgoolam International Airport, ensuring you arrive with ample time before your flight departure. Reflect on the incredible experiences and memories you've gathered during your stay in Mauritius as you bid farewell to this tropical paradise.

Day 5 is a day of cultural exploration and reflection, allowing you to appreciate the unique blend of nature, adventure, and heritage that defines Mauritius. As you depart for your onward journey, you'll carry with you not only souvenirs but also the warmth of the island's hospitality and the beauty of its landscapes in your heart.

This 5-day itinerary offers a well-rounded experience of Mauritius, covering its natural wonders, cultural heritage, and opportunities for adventure and relaxation. Adjust it according to your interests and preferences, and make sure to make reservations for activities and dining experiences in advance to ensure a smooth and memorable visit to this Indian Ocean gem.

## 7-day Travel itinerary

With its pristine beaches, lush landscapes, and vibrant culture, it's a dream destination for travelers seeking a perfect getaway. To make the most of your visit to Mauritius, here's a detailed 7-day travel itinerary that covers the island's diverse attractions and experiences.

Day 1: Arrival in Paradise
Morning:

- Arrive at Sir Seewoosagur Ramgoolam International Airport.

- Check into your chosen accommodation, whether it's a luxury resort, boutique hotel, or a cozy guesthouse.
- Freshen up and relax after your journey.

Afternoon:

- Head to the nearest beach for a leisurely swim or sunbathing.
- Explore the local area and get a feel for the island's atmosphere.
- Try some local street food or dine at your hotel.

Evening:

- Watch the sunset over the Indian Ocean - a breathtaking start to your journey.
- Enjoy a seafood dinner at a beachside restaurant.

Day 2: Discovering Port Louis
Morning:

- Drive to Port Louis, the capital city.
- Visit the bustling Central Market for a taste of Mauritian culture and shopping.
- Explore the Caudan Waterfront for shopping and dining options.

Afternoon:

- Discover the Aapravasi Ghat, a UNESCO World Heritage Site, and learn about the island's history.

- Visit the Blue Penny Museum to see rare stamps and artifacts.

Evening:

- Enjoy a delicious Creole dinner at a local restaurant.
- Explore the nightlife in Port Louis if you're in the mood for some entertainment.

Day 3: Beach Paradise - Grand Baie
Morning:

- Check out from your accommodation in Port Louis.
- Drive to Grand Baie, a lively beach town in the north.
- Check into your new lodging and unwind.

Afternoon:

- Spend your afternoon on the stunning Grand Baie Beach.
- Try water sports like snorkeling, paddleboarding, or parasailing.
- Explore the shops and cafes in the town.

Evening:

- Dine at a beachfront restaurant and savor fresh seafood.
- Enjoy the nightlife in Grand Baie, known for its vibrant bars and clubs.

Day 4: Cultural Exploration in Mahebourg
Morning:

- Leave Grand Baie and head to Mahebourg on the southeastern coast.
- Visit the Naval Museum and learn about the island's maritime history.
- Explore the Mahebourg Waterfront.

Afternoon:

- Have lunch at a local restaurant and savor Creole cuisine.
- Visit the historical site of Île aux Aigrettes to witness rare wildlife and conservation efforts.

Evening:

- Take a leisurely stroll along the Mahebourg waterfront.
- Savor a quiet dinner at a local eatery.

Day 5: Rodrigues Island Day Trip
Morning:

- Catch an early morning flight to Rodrigues Island.
- Explore this remote and unspoiled part of the Mauritian archipelago.
- Enjoy the pristine beaches, crystal-clear waters, and laid-back atmosphere.

Afternoon:

- Have lunch at a beachside café.
- Discover local culture and traditions by visiting the local markets and craft shops.

Evening:

- Return to Mauritius in the evening.
- Relax at your accommodation in Mahebourg.

Day 6: Natural Wonders of Mauritius
Morning:

- Head to the southern part of the island.
- Visit the Chamarel Seven Coloured Earth and Chamarel Waterfall.
- Explore Black River Gorges National Park, a haven for hiking and birdwatching.

Afternoon:

- Enjoy lunch at a local restaurant near the national park.
- Visit the Rhumerie de Chamarel for a rum tasting experience.

Evening:

- Return to your accommodation.

- Spend the evening at your leisure, perhaps with a spa treatment or a quiet dinner.

Day 7: Adventure and Farewell
Morning:

- Head to the adventure hub of the island, the Casela World of Adventures.
- Enjoy activities like ziplining, quad biking, and interacting with wildlife.

Afternoon:

- Have lunch at Casela or at a nearby restaurant.
- Explore La Vanille Nature Park to see giant tortoises and crocodiles.

Evening:

- Return to your accommodation for a relaxing evening.
- Have a farewell dinner, savoring your favorite Mauritian dishes.

Day 8: Departure from Paradise
Morning:

- Depending on your flight time, spend your last hours in Mauritius as you prefer.
- Consider some last-minute souvenir shopping.

Afternoon:

- Check out from your accommodation and head to the airport.
- Bid farewell to Mauritius with cherished memories.

This 7-day itinerary is a comprehensive guide to experiencing the best of Mauritius. However, feel free to adjust it based on your interests and the specific attractions you wish to explore on this enchanting island. Mauritius offers a wealth of experiences, whether you're seeking relaxation on its beaches, adventure in its jungles, or cultural immersion in its towns and cities. Enjoy your journey in this slice of paradise!

# Conclusion

In the heart of the Indian Ocean lies an island nation that truly encapsulates the essence of paradise – Mauritius. As we conclude our journey through this ultimate Mauritius travel companion, it is evident that this destination is more than just a spot on the world map; it is a world within itself, brimming with natural beauty, rich culture, and endless adventure.

Mauritius, often called the "Pearl of the Indian Ocean," has proven to be an unforgettable destination for travelers of all kinds. Whether you seek relaxation on pristine beaches, cultural immersion in bustling markets, thrilling exploration of lush jungles, or simply a taste of world-class cuisine, Mauritius has it all.

This travel guide has aimed to equip you with the knowledge and insight needed to make the most of your Mauritius experience. From the practical details of planning your trip to the enticing exploration of the island's regions, from choosing the perfect accommodation to indulging in its delectable cuisine, we've covered it all. We've delved into the rich tapestry of Mauritian culture and history, and we've showcased the breathtaking natural wonders that await your discovery.

Moreover, we've encouraged responsible tourism, emphasizing the importance of preserving this paradise for generations to come. Mauritius' delicate ecosystems and unique cultural heritage deserve our respect and protection.

As you prepare to embark on your Mauritius adventure, remember that this island is not just a destination; it's a journey that will leave an indelible mark on your heart and soul. Its people, landscapes, and experiences will stay with you long after your departure.

In the end, a trip to Mauritius is not just a vacation; it's an exploration of paradise. So, pack your bags, set your compass, and get ready to immerse yourself in the magic of Mauritius. Whether you're a seasoned traveler or a first-time explorer, this enchanting island offers something for everyone, and it's ready to welcome you with open arms.

Your adventure awaits, and the pages of this guide are your key to unlocking the treasures of Mauritius. So go forth, explore, savor, and create memories that will last a lifetime. As you take your first steps on this remarkable journey, remember that you are about to discover a paradise unlike any other – the incomparable paradise of Mauritius.

# Appendix A: Useful Phrases in Mauritian Creole

Mauritian Creole, locally known as "Kreol," is a vibrant and widely spoken language in Mauritius. While English and French are the official languages, knowing a few phrases in Mauritian Creole can greatly enhance your travel experience and help you connect with the locals. Here are some essential phrases and expressions to get you started:

Greetings and Common Phrases:

- Bonjour - Good morning.
- Bonswar - Good evening.
- Byen kontan fezer ou - Nice to meet you.
- Kouma ou santi ou? - How are you?
- Mo byen, mersi - I'm fine, thank you.
- Ki manyer ou apele? - What's your name?
- Mo apel... - My name is...
- Ki zour ou pou vini dan later? - When are you coming to the island?
- Ou bel - You're beautiful.
- Ki kot ou soti? - Where are you from?
- Mo sot de... - I come from...

Basic Conversational Phrases:
- Ki sa? - What is this?

- Mo pa konpran - I don't understand.
- Mo kontan ou ed mwa - I'm glad you're helping me.
- Kifer? - Why?
- Kot sa? - Where is that?
- Kan? - When?
- Komon? - How?

- Ki pri? - How much?
- Dimer! - Please!
- Mersi - Thank you.
- Ki ou rekonmand? - What do you recommend?
- Kontinie fer sa - Keep doing that.
- Ki pou manze? - What's for dinner?
- Graj - Delicious.

Emergency and Helpful Phrases:
- Ezitasyon! - Help!

- Kot la siris? - Where is the hospital?
- Mo bezwen dokter - I need a doctor.
- Ki non ou? - What's your name?
- Kontakte polis - Call the police.
- Banny zwen dan sa direksyon la - They went that way.
- Fe sa vit - Do it quickly.
- Mo pe santi mwa malad - I'm feeling sick.

Numbers:
- Zero - Zero

- Enn - One
- De - Two
- Troa - Three
- Kat - Four
- Sank - Five
- Sis - Six
- Set - Seven
- Wit - Eight
- Nef - Nine
- Dis - Ten

Days of the Week:

- Dimans - Sunday

- Lendi - Monday
- Mardi - Tuesday
- Merkredi - Wednesday
- Zedi - Thursday
- Vandredi - Friday
- Samdi - Saturday

Months of the Year:
- Janvie - January

- Fevriye - February
- Mars - March
- Avril - April
- Me - May
- Zwen - June
- Ziyet - July
- Out - August
- Septam - September
- Oktob - October
- Novam - November
- Desam – December

When visiting Mauritius, you may find it helpful to have language translation apps on your smartphone to assist with communication, especially if you're not fluent in French or English. Here are three popular language translation apps that can be useful:

Google Translate:
- Google Translate is a widely used and trusted translation app. It supports over 100 languages, including French and English, which are commonly spoken in Mauritius.

- You can use it to translate text, speech, and even images. Simply point your camera at a sign or menu, and it can translate it for you.
- Google Translate also offers a conversation mode, where two people can speak into the app, and it will translate their conversation in real-time.

iTranslate:
- iTranslate is a user-friendly translation app that supports over 100 languages and dialects. It's available on both iOS and Android devices.
- This app offers text and voice translation, making it easy to communicate with locals. You can also switch between languages quickly and save your favorite phrases for offline access.

Microsoft Translator:
- Microsoft Translator is a versatile translation app available for both iOS and Android. It supports a wide range of languages, including French and English.
- One standout feature is the conversation mode, which allows for real-time translation between two people speaking different languages. It's great for on-the-fly communication.
- Microsoft Translator also offers offline translation for some languages, which can be helpful when you're in areas with limited internet connectivity.

Remember to download the necessary language packs or ensure that you have an internet connection when using these apps in Mauritius. Having one of these translation apps on hand can greatly assist you in navigating the island and engaging with locals more effectively.

# Appendix B: Traveler's Checklist

Before embarking on your journey to Mauritius, it's essential to be well-prepared. This checklist will help ensure you have everything in order for a smooth and enjoyable trip:

Travel Documents:

- Passport (valid for at least six months beyond your planned departure)
- Visa (if required, check with the Mauritian embassy or consulate)
- Travel insurance (including medical coverage)
- Copies of important documents (passport, insurance, travel itinerary)

Health and Safety:

- Vaccinations and medications (consult with your healthcare provider)
- First-aid kit (band-aids, antiseptic, pain relievers)
- Mosquito repellent and sunscreen
- Emergency contact information

Packing Essentials:

- Lightweight clothing suitable for warm weather
- Swimwear and beachwear
- Comfortable walking shoes
- Electrical adapters and converters
- Mobile phone and charger

Finances:

- Sufficient cash (Mauritian Rupees) or credit/debit cards
- Notify your bank of your travel plans to avoid card issues abroad
- Small bills for tips and local purchases

Travel Accessories:

- Travel guidebook or digital travel apps
- Travel pillow and eye mask for long flights
- Travel-sized toiletries
- Snacks for the journey

Electronics:

- Camera and accessories
- Smartphone and charger
- Power bank
- Travel adapters and voltage converters

Miscellaneous:

- Travel lock and cable ties for luggage security
- Travel-sized laundry detergent (if washing clothes on the go)
- Reusable water bottle
- Any necessary prescription medications

Remember to tailor this checklist to your personal needs and preferences, and make sure to double-check it before your departure to ensure a hassle-free vacation in Mauritius.

# Appendix C: Recommended Reading and Resources

To enhance your understanding of Mauritius and make the most of your trip, here is a list of recommended reading materials and online resources:

Books:

- "Mauritius - Culture Smart!: The Essential Guide to Customs & Culture" by Tom Phillips
- "Mauritius: Rodrigues, Réunion" by Dana Facaros and Michael Pauls
- "Lonely Planet Mauritius, Réunion & Seychelles" by Lonely Planet
- "The Rough Guide to Mauritius" by Rough Guides
- "Mauritius: Isle of Contrasts" by Alain P. Pollet

Websites:

Mauritius Tourism Promotion Authority (https://tourism.govmu.org/Pages/Authorities%20and%20Board/newMPTA.aspx)

Mauritius Travel (https://www.tripadvisor.com/Attractions-g293816-Activities-Mauritius.html)

TripAdvisor Mauritius (https://www.tripadvisor.com/Tourism-g293816-Mauritius-Vacations.html)

Mauritius Explored (https://mauritiusexplored.com/)

Blogs and Travel Journals:

MyMauritiusTravel (https://mymauritius.travel/)

MauritiusConscious (https://www.mauritiusconscious.com/)

Travel Forums:

- Lonely Planet Thorn Tree - Mauritius Forum
- TripAdvisor Mauritius Forums

These resources will provide you with valuable insights, travel tips, and up-to-date information about Mauritius, ensuring that you have a memorable and enriching experience on the island.

Printed in Great Britain
by Amazon